CIRCULATION ROTA

CW01246150

WITHDRAWN FROM STOCK

THE BATTLE OF EL ALAMEIN
AND BEYOND

THE BATTLE OF EL ALAMEIN AND BEYOND

G. A. Morris

The Book Guild Ltd.
Sussex, England.

This book is sold subject to the condition that it shall not, by way of trade or otherwise, be lent, re-sold, hired out, photocopied or held in any retrieval system or otherwise circulated without the publisher's prior consent in any form of binding or cover other than that in which this is published and without a similar condition including this condition being imposed on the subsequent purchaser.

The Book Guild Ltd.
25 High Street,
Lewes, Sussex

First published 1993
© G. A. Morris 1993
Set in Baskerville
Typesetting by Southern Reproductions (Sussex)
East Grinstead, Sussex
Printed in Great Britain by
Antony Rowe Ltd.
Chippenham, Wiltshire.

A catalogue record for this book is
available from the British Library

ISBN 0 86332 626 9

CONTENTS

Foreword		7
Chapter 1	Prelude – The Road to Dunkirk	9
Chapter 2	The Desert War – Early Campaigns	29
Chapter 3	The Battle of El Alamein	47
Chapter 4	On To Tunis	66
Chapter 5	The Invasion of Europe	80
Chapter 6	Following the Sun	98
Chapter 7	Out to Grass	172
Appendix One	An Exercise in History	180
Appendix Two	The Demon Drink	185
Appendix Three	A Secret Interlude	188
List of Illustrations		190

To those gallant, ill-used, half-starved and flogged sailors and soldiers and their unsurpassed leaders Nelson and Wellington. Probably the finest fighting forces ever assembled, successful in a twenty-two year long struggle against the would-be world conqueror, Napoleon.

Also to their descendants who by the magnificent operation in the Falklands gave such a boost to the British morale.

FOREWORD

Studying for a Ph.D. degree with a major in History I submitted as a demonstration of professional expertise, my recollections of this important battle in the Second World War. At the time I was asked to enlarge this dissertation to book length, but tired from a year long arduous labour, I declined.

Subsequently I decided to carry on purely for self-satisfaction not for any other particular motive.

The narrative covers other parts of the war and subsequent peace time activities, including other conflicts then encountered.

Few names no pack drill.

G. A. Morris

1

PRELUDE – THE ROAD TO DUNKIRK

History, the story of the past, events centred around wars of political and religious origins; kings, queens and dictators; greed and famine; creed and colours. Having lived for more than three-quarters of the twentieth century I find myself increasingly contemplating the historical events of that period, with the realization that we live in history.

Why Alamein? Study of the Napoleonic wars leads one to the inevitable connection Napoleon – Hitler and in some sense Pitt – Churchill. Both Boney and Adolf aimed at world conquest, through Russia and Egypt, both defeated for the first time in their great pincer thrusts to the East. By comparison we have Corruna and Moscow as turning-points in the twenty-two year long Napoleonic war.

EARLY YEARS

Born at the very beginning of the Great War to end all wars, my middle name Antwerp, coming into the world the same day as an uncle was killed at that place during the Royal Marines' raid on the Belgian coast. First names were very subscribed by those of reigning monarchs, thousands of Victorias, Alberts, Edwards, Georges and Marys. North End village, Hampstead, town and country was paradise in which to grow up, full of nature; trees, grass, birds, particularly, and wild flowers, many superb walks and a beautiful park with a few deer, bears, ducks, swans, moorhens and peacocks. A great place for lovers and popular for open air love-making, so pitiful to see couples escorted to the police station by park or heath keepers or policemen, no squad cars, but there was a two-wheeled cart for transporting suicides, gruesomely covered by stiff tarpaulins. I did once find a man with his throat cut. Apparently he failed to sever his jugular vein and was carted away bubbling blood through an open wind-pipe.

THE GREAT WAR

My very earliest memories were mostly of the war, scenes which are curiously sharpened by age and could not be imagined. I believe this is a common phenomenon. Being wheeled in my pram, looking up at the stars, to a cellar beneath a mansion in Golders Hill Park, a tunnel-like shelter with practically the whole village assembled. The mansion was destroyed in 1940 by a sea mine parachuted from a German bomber; the mine landed in a tree and the explosion neatly sliced off the upper parts of most of the village houses. I recall seeing Zeppelins at night caught in searchlight beams, long silvery cigar shapes, quite beautiful and not at all sinister; the same in daylight which must have been the daylight raid on London; anti-aircraft fire certainly, with shrapnel pelting down; the airship falling in flames at Cuffley shot down by an RFC pilot, Capt. Ball(?). A Russian émigré-countess, whom my father told me later was named Violet Zebanski, abducted me from my pram, I was then three years of age and can clearly see the rather austere lady with a great flowered hat and smelling of patchouli. The police recovered me after three days. The summer of 1921 very clear, rockets being shot in the air to produce rain to break a severe drought, failed of course, as well bring tribal rainmakers! The Sinn Fein were very active then and we children dug trenches in our sand-pit to repel them, armed with sticks and broom handles. I had an old broken Daisy air-rifle, the most coveted weapon. First being carted reluctantly off to school by my sisters and not behaving myself at all well.

THE VILLAGE

Many great houses and mansions, a few cottages, terraced

villas, three public houses, compacted by the entirely surrounding Heath and I suppose still is today. Our lowly cottage, one of three, on the Heath, served by a granite paved footpath from a cul-de-sac where there was a small church and school. My mother attended this school and stayed on to teach until she married at around thirty years of age, when I suppose the school closed as we went to another one in Hampstead itself.

The cottage had four rooms and a scullery complete with copper boiler, outside toilet, diminutive garden and tiny yard, six shillings a week rent and of course the landlord simply could not afford to carry out any repairs. The poor in those days could not do other than rent houses at very low sums with ever more unwilling owners leading to the current arrangement of private ownership and mortgages, perhaps not so satisfactory. A relaxation of rent controls might have avoided this modern millstone. Some few years after the

My Mother and some of her children. Myself held by Mother – probably 1916 – in the village school playground.

Second World War I was offered the repaired cottage, from the land-sea mine damage, for £22,000, subsequently it was bought by a very well-known actor and today would realize probably some £100,000 plus. My parents, and at one time, seven children, shared three bedrooms, and the tiny kitchen was always overcrowded. Bath night once a week, tin bath fed from the copper, shared with our cousins next door, the same water of course with a bit of hot added occasionally. The boys and girls were separated but probably that was when we became aware of the missing parts. My mother, however, was very strict with our cleanliness and general hygiene, father cut our hair, nails and cleaned shoes.

There were four famous public houses, the Old Bull and Bush of music hall fame sung by Florrie Ford; The Hare and Hounds, bombed in 1940 and the rebuilt; Jack Straw's Castle of Wat Tyler's day; The Spaniards Inn, with highwayman Dick Turpin associations. All very popular especially when the Hampstead Fair was there for Bank Holidays; at these holidays crowds came from the East End of London, so-called costermongers, bringing with them police from the relevant divisions, big, burly, beery men able to handle the unruly crowds. Much drunkenness, fighting, even between women; gangs of hundreds of youths from different districts pitched battles with sticks, stones and bottles. Exciting but tragic, a safety valve from their grim lives. One feature of village life was the drying ground, known as the 'lines', where women hung out the washing, done in the coppers, and met to chat. In winter, which seemed much colder than now, all pipes froze up and water was collected from the village pump; skating and tobogganing every year. Very few cars mostly horses and carts, glorious steam engines at the Fair, all polished brass.

OUR NEIGHBOURS

There were the poor and the illustrious, very rich aristocrats and notables. My father was a minor civil servant, told many of his experiences as messenger to, among others, Lloyd George and Winston Churchill whom he heartily disliked but thought Lady Churchill very gracious. He retired finally from the Patents Office Library and finished his days in Surbiton, going there after the North End cottage was bombed. We were not exactly poor and starving but in the eyes of our rich neighbours we qualified, with the other 'poor', for coals and blankets at Christmas. With a family of seven we inevitably inherited the older children's worn clothes. My first long trousers were an old pair of my father's. I well remember my maternal grandmother, a fearsome old lady, long grey woollen skirts and army boots, she used to hit out at me with her walking stick. I was quite naughty as are most boys, among other things smashed the WC bowl with a hammer and also set fire to the kitchen, the only times my father smacked me. They were very good parents and I appreciated them very much more in retrospect when they died. It is worth having a look at those aforementioned great ones in some detail.

OUR ILLUSTRIOUS NEIGHBOURS

The Earl of Clarendon our nearest neighbour, lived in William Pitt's house. I cannot recollect ever having seen him.

Lord Leverhulme of Sunlight Soap had a glorious house and gardens, several Rolls in the garages. Later this house was the property of Lord Inverclyde, who, if my memory serves me correctly, married Jessie Matthews, a glorious wedding; she was extremely beautiful.

Lady Hoare. My Godmother; aunt of Sir Samuel Hoare, later Lord Templewood, Viceroy of India. She was very good to me but refused to pass on a letter of application for a position with the Viceroy until I could write a decent letter. She did in fact procure me a job, even during the terrible depression.

The Webbs. Great Socialists, friends of H G Wells, went with H G in the 20s to see Lenin. Sidney Webb was invalided and used a three-wheel pony trap which he could steer by a handle turning the front wheel and pressuring the pony to move right or left.

Frank Salisbury, the painter.

General Stockton. A descendant of a General Stockton

renowned in the Peninsula War. His military funeral was most impressive, led by his charger, jackboots reversed in the stirrups.

Lady Houston. A very rich eccentric old lady, not so simple, a widow of three husbands all of whom left her large sums of money. She used to drive out in a beautiful open Rolls Royce with a tame pet monkey on a lead.

Rabbi Mattuck. The Chief Rabbi in England. Had a charming daughter and was very kind to us poor children.

Anna Pavlova had a lovely manor house. I used to climb her garden wall to see her sometimes practising in the garden.

Olive Sainsbury had a nearby very expensive mansion.

Sir Arthur Conan Doyle, creator of Sherlock Holmes – we often met walking on the Heath, cloaked and with a broad-brimmed hat, like a sombrero.

Sir Oliver Lodge, spiritualist. Cannot recall having seen him.

The Du Mauriers. My mother claimed to have been well-acquainted with either George or Gerald, very likely as I have been told that when young she was very beautiful. My father sometimes referred to her not so blameless past. I often saw and passed the time of day with Daphne Du Maurier and her sister, such lovely young ladies. Lord Weir of pump fame and Guiness of stout. There were other such notables whom I have forgotten; strangely no middle-class. The poor were farm labourers, carpenters, bricklayers, gardeners, domestic servants, stablemen and chauffeurs. There were two small shops, a dairy and a sweet and tobacco confectioners, both destroyed in 1940. The shopkeeper had worked in the Argentine on railways construction and had some interesting tales. The butcher, baker and milkman delivered daily, milk in churns scooped into your jug. A good place in which to grow up; but for having lost my home there I would surely have remained in the village after leaving the Army in 1948 instead of living and working in so many foreign parts; all our uncles, aunts, cousins left in 1940 and few acquaintances remained.

SCHOOL DAYS

Myself and two sisters were left in 1918 out of our family of seven. I went to the nearest parochial school, escorted by my sisters, rather older than usual as I refused to wear trousers and remained in frocks, the normal small boys' dress, until forced into shorts and school. Of course to begin with it was play and toys. Being a mixed school the interesting difference in the sexes arose. Boys were to be seen playing with themselves concealed by their desks; we were all in love with a beautiful young lady teacher and tried very hard to see up her skirts, which were, as I remember, quite short. My father taught me history and geography, his methodology was ideal and I believe is currently being recommended for schools; 1066 Battle of Hastings, William the Norman Conqueror, Hastings, King Harold, arrow in the eye, building up an unforgettable mind picture. For geography, a country, its capital, rivers, mountains, people, climate, monarchy. One teacher at school was an ex-Canadian infantry soldier, four years in the trenches where the Canadians bore more than a fair share of the fighting. In the early twenties we had a crystal-set radio, which my father constructed, a crystal of galena activated by a cat's whisker, fine copper-wire; the sound coming from a pudding basin containing the ear-phones. A great relief was to have a one-valve receiver with a loudspeaker, but we had to be as quiet as mice. We have never had much luck with the BBC in spite of their optimistic reports of improved world reception and technological advances. Once caught up in the 1967 Arab-Israeli war we could not raise the BBC over the critical six days. Even now in Cyprus I am frequently reminded of our pudding basin days, in 1990! At thirteen I achieved a scholarship from the LCC, a magnificent £50 per annum with free books, very generous, out of which I managed to start a lifetime habit of saving and getting interest. I attended the Polytechnic Secondary School in Regent Street, bicycling the six miles each way, sometimes by Underground when the weather was very bad, even then entailing a mile and a half walk to the station and best part of a mile the other end. We were worked very hard, hours of homework, to write a poem at weekends was purgatory. Matriculation at fifteen in eight subjects, Higher Schools

Intermediate degree at eighteen. My French was poor so I had extra tuition by a cousin, headmistress of a girls' school until she went on exchange to Canada. Then a young, nubile wife of one of my father's colleagues tutored me and I will always remember her lessons. In the course of my life I perforce became quite fluent in French, German and Arabic with bits of other languages coming in useful. My secret, apart from learning in bed was to write down, learn and use five words a day.

EMPLOYMENT

Now the 1929 Depression was on and very depressing it was; so affected by the situation I decided to quit school and go to work and with my Godmother's help I was taken on by a small engineering company in Berners Street near the Middlesex Hospital, of which she was a shareholder. We were kept very hard at the drawing-board, no smoking, no tea breaks, twenty-five shillings a week for three years; evening classes at the Borough and Northern Polytechnics. However, then success came with a magnificent seven pounds a week, in those days a very good salary. Between the wars there was a very good time for Britain, a land of increasing prosperity for all. I had the best and fastest motorcycles and a small ancient car, money for pleasures and substantial additions to the bank account. During schooldays and afterwards I visited France, Germany, Holland and Belgium with many memorable incidents. Between leaving school and employment I spent a little time at the Cité Universitaire, Brussels and the Haut Ecole des Mines at Liége. In September 1938 I was on holiday in Germany at the same time as the umbrella'd Prime Minister, a seemingly pathetic figure with his announcement 'Peace in our time', following his meeting with Hitler. France and Britain gave way too easily to the aggressive Hitler. When I returned after my holiday, staggered by the all-present German troops, SS and Brown Shirts, yellow-starred Jews, I joined the Territorial Army, the Royal Engineers at the Duke of York's HQ, Chelsea; it was suggested I apply for a commission but decided against this. Time-consuming, it led to a break with my lady friend who on parting said, 'You have wasted five years of my life'. A very lovely girl, red-gold hair and green eyes, born for love as such females are, desired by many men. However there were plenty of girls to be had. The army very rapidly turned us into something like soldiers, quite remarkable, producing martial responses to the obviously approaching war. Holidaying in Jersey in August 1939, I received my mobilisation papers and returned home on an already blacked-out steamer with a destroyer on patrol. The beginning of a new era.

THE PHONEY WAR

So before war was declared we were more or less settled down in a Chelsea Square of large empty houses, straw-filled palliasses the first chore, bare boards and nothing else. Sunday morning 3 September 1939 at 11.00 war was declared and the sirens went. Great panic, we were herded indoors and screamed at for looking up at the sky, the enemy airmen would see our white faces! I was then a Corporal, a good rank, as that of Captain, avoidance of many unpleasant duties and less responsibility, a rank I held until commissioned; there is a barrier step Corporal to Sergeant, Captain to Major. So we gradually gathered kit and equipment, were medically examined, including stick parade which involved the MO in raising one's penis with his swagger cane, being inoculated and vaccinated. Many strong men fainted at the sight of the needle going in. I was employed teaching NCOs to ride motorcycles, absolutely hilarious the ensuing antics, a rather unpleasant sergeant dragging his feet along the ground to stop with damaging results to man and machine.

We moved to Hurst Park Racecourse at the end of September, mostly employed in the processes of just living, little time for training. I did meet up with a girl I knew well before, very intimately in fact, but she was not keen on soldiers; at that time soldiers of the Regular Army, having joined of necessity were not, shall we say, drawing-room types.

THE BEF IN FRANCE

In October we were off to France. The four mile march to the railway station was an incredible, unforgettable feat; change of quarter order which meant all one possessed, large and small packs, rifle and bayonet, fifty rounds of ammunition, waterbottle, ground-sheet, two blankets, gas mask, full kitbag, steel helmet, etc., etc. It never happened to us again, but what a simple way to move troops without using any transport. An uneventful sea voyage to Le Havre where on arrival I was detailed to drive a Humber staff car out of the docks to a vehicle park. On the wrong side of the road I crashed head-on into an oncoming French civilian car. I am sorry to say that I just scarpered back to my unit and never heard a word of the affair again. So back to 1914-18, railway trucks labelled 40 hommes, 8 chevals. A ghastly journey, tins of water, bully beef and biscuits, intermittent halts and finally spewing out at a small station on the Belgian border, Auchy near Lille, where we were to remain until May 1940. Our Major called for French speakers, two of us stepped out. We went round the village with a French officer, allocating so many men to this barn, that ruined cottage, the Officers' Mess, the Sergeants' Mess. All very grim, cold, wet and filthy, food unfit for pigs, much disease occurred, scabies particularly, lice, rats abundant and on top of that misery an outbreak of influenza. The mentality was entirely founded on trench warfare, based on the previous war; we were engaged in extending the Maginot Line along the Belgian frontier to the coast. I mostly spent my time on Railway Transport Officer's duties at the quite extensive yards near Auchy. To reach these I used to march down the railway line and one morning met the whole of the BEF General Staff coming in the opposite direction, the Duke of Gloucester, Lord Gort and his generals, Montgomery as commander 3 INF DIV was surely there; beautifully turned out, brasses, boots, spurs, red tabs and hat-bands and polished Sam-Browne belts. Myself, miserable Corporal, the awful shapeless brown overalls we were issued with then and the impossible forage cap, saluting all the way down the line and having my salute returned. Our first company bath parade I will never forget, two halves of a hogs-head barrel filled with water which quickly became a filthy grey slimy mess as we dipped one after the other. Afterwards we acquired some company transport and went to the public baths in Douai, where an old woman would bang on the door if we were more than a few minutes. We also went to the cinema in Douai, the town attractively blued-out as opposed to the British black-out. On one such occasion I went to start the truck, nothing happened, opened the bonnet, no engine; whoever stole it must have had a crane. No women, except once to an enormous brothel in Lille, a quite unforgettable experience. A sapper deserted on this jaunt and when he was caught by the MPs I was sent to bring him back, he was not punished, he was an alcoholic and our major was a very understanding man. This particular sapper rolled drunkenly off the back of a truck in flaming Poperinghe on our way out when the balloon went up, never heard of again. Compared with the *poilu* we were very well paid, a similar difference between the British and Americans, later on.

Beset with scabies, ringworm and an obscure fever, most likely swine-fever as we were living like pigs, I spent some days in a vile place called a Casualty Clearing Station, housed in an old brewery; one of the patients, in despair I suppose, blew his brains out with a sleeping guard's rifle. The spring of 1940 was very pleasant and there were lovely walks to be enjoyed, good cheap beers and wines in the village estaminets and always oeufs frittes. In January I had seven days home leave, travelled this time in full marching order, that is only minus kitbag, festooned like a Christmas tree, barely able to sit down, eyed askance by civilians, herded out of the main line stations by MPs. It was a good leave mostly spent in the West End chasing the girls with some success when out of uniform. Lyons Corner Houses served a very good steak and strong Bass beer and one evening having such a meal, I was joined by an obvious serviceman who turned out to be a Petty Officer from *HMS Ajax,* fresh from the sinking of the *Graf Spee* off Montevideo. We were picked up by two very generous young ladies who provided us with a one-night entertainment in their flat. The PO and I parted very good comrades.

At five am 10 May 1940 it began, the phoney war was over, many bombers flew over and dropped bombs on nearby towns. There obviously was some sort of plan for us, but it seemed to appear very vague; however we moved off into

Belgium where I was detached with a few sappers to operate an Engineer Stores dump, obviously set up before Belgium was invaded by the Germans.

At around the end of December 1939 we were visited by King George VI, lined up for several hours in the freezing cold and snow, fortunately we had been issued with very fine leather jerkins, which I am wearing at this moment and have used continually, a present from our King, a fondly-remembered monarch. He drove by in a closed Daimler limousine, looking a little miserable as we also were. So I ran the dump, not many customers and no contact with my company. It became very obvious that whatever fighting there was going on was getting nearer and there was movement in the wrong direction, backwards. An officer came by one day, a captain of the Black Watch, with a miscellaneous bunch of about fifty soldiers, mostly Cameronians, he suggested we join him, which I did. Well we tramped back through Belgium into France stopping at farmhouses abandoned by the population. Cows were left with the names of the owners marked on boards wired to their horns; very pitiful they were, mooing to be milked, which we obliged them when able. Once cooking some chickens and potatoes in buckets at a small farmhouse the family returned, the Germans had pierced the Maginot Line and had thus surrounded the north of France, the fleeing populace were obliged to turn round.

Our airforce was busy fighting a losing battle using ancient Gladiators against Messerschmitt 109s. I saw three shot down nearby, all we found were deep holes with the engines at the bottom and one service tunic miraculously intact, a Wing-Commander with a string of medals from the 1914-18 war. We also saw German paratroops machine-gunned in the air; not very chivalrous. We had been warned to look out for the 5th column infiltrators, possibly disguised as nuns! Shades of the stories rife about atrocities in Belgium in 1914. On a lonely stroll I did encounter a man up a tree flashing a mirror. I have often considered since, what on earth for? He jumped down and ran, I caught him and in the struggle I am sorry to say I used my sheath-knife too effectively. He had the mirror, a pair of nail scissors and a box of cheese segments on him only, no weapon, no papers. The scissors and the knife were in use until 1974 when they were liberated by Turkish soldiers, among many other things, during the invasion of Cyprus.

DUNKIRK

During the retreat, which we did not know as such, no idea what was going on, the same group led by the gallant captain, halted in small hamlets and took up defensive positions with one Bren machine gun. On two occasions the enemy flashed through on motorcycles and armoured cars completely ignoring us. Water was the main problem, food did not matter, but we were ever thirsty in the hot days of early summer. Most of our kit had been systematically discarded to end up in a light battle order. After a week of marching we picked up some lorries whose drivers did not seem to know where to go either. We once passed a column of German tanks going the other way. Fortunately they showed no interest in us. We arrived at St Malo-les-Bains, seven miles from Dunkirk, joined by a fine beach and sand-dunes. Seeing a glorious red-tabbed Staff Officer I politely asked him what was happening, he completely ignored me!

Entering a house at night looking for water a voice called, 'Who's there?' When I answered he said, 'I know you.' It was the Black Watch Captain, blinded by bomb blast. He would not come with me, saying, 'My life is soldiering and now it is finished.' Sorrowfully I left him behind.

The sight of the beach was appalling, a queue of soldiers some ten deep stretching darkly against the golden sand; an enormous plume of black smoke from the burning oil storage tanks at Dunkirk. We then realized the situation and were astonished that we had been defeated so easily. So we joined the end of the queue, bombed, shelled and machine-gunned, unable to leave our places as there was definitely no return only to go back to the end. Many small boats arrived off-shore and were swamped by crowds of men wading out to them. I do not know how many days it took to reach the harbour at Dunkirk but eventually we arrived. Word had been passed along the beach to remove the bolts from our rifles and throw them into the sea and abandon the rifles. A nonsensical order, no difficulty to carry our arms whatever happened. It turned out afterwards that there was an extreme shortage of small arms and the Home Guard was armed with broomsticks for drill purposes. Later on I was in charge of an operation delivering small-arms throughout Britain with small vans, a Carter Paterson service with routes advised by the AA.

The harbour was a shambles, under constant divebombing, sunken ships everywhere. We lay on the mole it seemed for hours, waiting for a ship. An RN Captain wearing his soft cap with scrambled egg peak, stood calmly on the sea wall directing operations. In a lull I went over to him and said 'Sir, I don't know how you do it.'

He replied, 'Navy training, old boy, and you look as though you could do with a square meal!' He was only the third officer I encountered during the retreat and many soldiers were not pleased with the apparent lack of leadership. Finally an old British Railway cross-channel steamer came alongside, the SS *Canterbury,* and no time was lost getting on board; a destroyer was sunk close by as we embarked. Bombed and hit on the way over to Dover, but not seriously. We saw a smartly turned out RSM just jump into the sea during the attack.

After writing the above I came across an article published in *The Times* of 12 May 1990 commemorating the fiftieth anniversary of the Dunkirk episode, headed – 'Better shot at than lose your place'. How true! The half page reproduction of a painting by Charles Cundall, 'The Withdrawal from Dunkirk, June 1940', original at The Imperial War Museum, London, portrays the scene very realistically. Compares with other battle paintings such as 'The Retreat from Moscow', 'The Charge of the Light Brigade' and 'Waterloo' among others, perhaps not so powerful but in the same category.

A SPELL IN ENGLAND

A period followed in England of being shunted around from camp to camp, almost living in trains, not allowed leave as feelings were high among the troops who considered the whole campaign a fiasco, which it obviously was. We were never informed of intentions, etc. of the BEF compared to subsequent operation, particularly under Monty, when every soldier knew what was going on and what was expected of him. Finally the RE company was united at Barnsley in Yorkshire, disciplined by a special QMSI Warrant Officer, a very highly qualified instructor and drill martinet. Some of us were selected to become officers; most of our original officers and NCOs were not seen by us again, a great weeding out had taken place after Dunkirk. At the first camp outside Blandford in Dorset I met up with our Despatch Rider who was barely able to walk; when I looked at his leg he had a terrible wound – most of the muscle being torn away – a bullet hitting his motorcycle had driven the smashed cylinder into his leg. He was afraid to report to the MO in case his leg would be amputated; I brought the MO to him and off he went on a stretcher.

OFFICER TRAINING AND COMMISSION

The Officer Cadet Training Unit (OCTU), was housed in a very old Naval Barracks between Portsmouth and Southsea, Victoria Barracks, if I remember correctly, probably dated back to the Napoleonic wars. One of the cadets was from the Royal Tanks and had been in Calais. This regiment I later joined and learned a regimental ballad by our chronicler, part of which went:

> They gave me an A.10* and I drove her
> From Fordingbridge on to the train,
> We matelot'd to Calais from Dover
> and soon matelot'd back home again.
>
> *Chorus –*
> Oh, I wear a green tab** on my shoulder
> and a little white tank on my arm
> 'Twas the Third Tanks that taught me to soldier
> and with them I will come to no harm.

---

* The A.10 was a light tank designed for cavalry roles.
** Green Tab – each of the eight regular tank battalions wore a distinctive colour ribbon on shoulder straps.

September was very lively indeed culminating for us in the destruction of the barracks during the night of 17 - 18 September when the attempted German invasion took place. As in 1804 when Napoleon also tried to invade Britain, the landing craft, barges, were damaged by the high seas and on both occasions the Royal Navy action. It was reported that many bodies were washed ashore along the Channel coasts.

This particular night I was on watch atop a high tower, most unpleasant, it swayed from the blast of the bombs. We moved off to peaceful Leicester and after a tough period of hard work and the constant threat of being Returned to Unit as unsuitable (it never happened), passed out as 2nd Lieutenants.

General Montgomery inspected us at the passing out parade.

Now if Corporals and Captains have a good spot in the military hierarchy, then 2nd Lieutenants have the worst, absolute dogsbodies! I am afraid I was rebellious, often on the carpet and finally posted off to the desert, which is what I wanted anyway.

My first posting was to Weedon small-arms depot and the aforementioned Carter Paterson Service. The Commanding Officer, a full Colonel, was then the oldest serving officer with a commission of some fifty-one years, a very charming likeable officer. There I met and courted a very beautiful American girl who had joined the ATS. She followed me later to the Middle East but we failed to meet.

Next I was posted to a Tank Regiment under training at Otley in Yorkshire, with the new Churchill tanks, later moving to Eastbourne and my expulsion to foreign climes. It was an amusing period, could fill a whole book with hilarious incidents, a good life for a young officer used to the ill-usage and approaching two pips, another not so bad rank.

OFF TO WAR AGAIN

To Liverpool and the *Windsor Castle,* a fine passenger liner of the Union Castle Line, still then in her peacetime glory. We were to sail to Egypt via the Cape, as the Med was out except for Malta convoys. Our convoy was mixed with cargo ships and the inevitable destroyer escort; one large battleship a six inch AA gun cruiser sailed in the middle of the convoy, as we remarked we seemed to be taking care of her. Our OC Troops was one of three brothers, all troopers; on his first boat drill he asked me if I had a revolver and ammunition and detailed me to a station on the main companion way with orders to shoot if necessary to prevent panic, I often wonder what would have happened. There were many buzzes as we proceeded southwards; we were going to India; to the Pacific and anywhere but our actual destination. At Freetown a great hoax was played on us, a notice posted to the effect that a dance was to be held on another liner, rumoured to have service women on board, boats leaving at 19.00. So a great scurry to get out best uniforms, sam-browne belts, brass polishing etc, all in an impossibly hot and humid air. A truly magnificent leg-pull, we were all fooled.

SOUTH AFRICA

There was a young woman on board, reputed to be a secretary to Casey who was a special government official in Cairo. She bestowed her favours on a most unprepossessing officer, one can never tell! However, she was put ashore at Freetown, reputed to be a spy. We sailed off down the South Atlantic; saw some spouting whales; several alarms but no hostile activity in evidence. We were landed at Cape Town to await another ship northward bound. We were very well taken care of by the South Africans particularly the girls who were rather different from those we were accustomed to, more forthcoming and hard drinkers, but it seemed not particularly promiscuous. One young lady accosted me when shopping in Adderley Street for a pocket flask, which she found and insisted on paying for; went to her home for dinner, her father a very rich shipping magnate, however, mother definitely disapproved. I took an instant dislike to Apartheid, confirmed after two unpleasant incidents. We were housed in a camp outside Cape Town and were allocated African batmen. My boy was an extremely nice helpful Basuto. I was very angry when a South African sergeant booted him for absolutely no reason. Having a dinner party at a very exclusive restaurant where our hostess was said to be a very affluent person of good family, two policemen appeared at the table and ordered her out, more or less at gun-point; she was one-sixteenth coloured. Of course Apartheid was present in all activities everywhere one went. Offered a very good job in South Africa after the war I refused unhesitatingly, although I knew it would have been a wonderful life. Now in 1990 one must say 'was it worth it?' Apartheid, Stalinism, the Berlin Wall, all follies.

EGYPT

We travelled on after a short stay, up the Indian Ocean on a small, somewhat dilapidated steamer *Scythia*, which was sunk on the way back. The problem in the Indian Ocean was Japanese submarines, not aircraft. One memorable sight was *Queen Mary* rushing by, unescorted because of her superior speed, said to be thirty-three knots. We had some nurses on the *Scythia* and I was fortunate to become very friendly with a Red Cross nurse, a rather superior young woman who later used to send me things up the 'blue', the blue being the desert. We did meet up once in Alexandria and when the regiment returned to England she wrote saying, 'You never went to see Daddy as you promised.' Daddy was a retired Admiral living near the New Forest. I befriended the ship's carpenter and acquired bits of wood from him which I carved into various toys and ornaments, which certainly went down with the *Scythia*. We arrived at Suez and disembarked at Port Tewfik; in the dark I walked into some dannert barbed wire which did not do my legs much good. The train to Cairo was very civilised, wagon-lits standard and one could obtain drinks. We shared a table with a major who had been in Egypt since 1936 and when a sudden stop upset our drinks he said that if the driver had done that in the old days he would have been thrashed. The Royal Armoured Corps were housed in a very old barracks just outside Cairo at Abbasiya.

It now became apparent that the convoy and the barracks was comprised mainly of junior officers, among whom casualties were very high. The colonel interviewed all newly joined officers and decided their postings; he was a very

3rd Royal Tanks badge.
Inset 11th Armoured div. Bashing Bull and 4th Armoured Desert Rat.

elegant 7th Hussar. I was to remain at the depot for the time being as an instructor in the Driving and Maintenance wing, which with Gunnery and Wireless extra training, were endeavouring to ensure that personnel bound for regiments were hopefully capable of joining the fight. The situation in the desert in January 1942 was very grim for the British. Rommel's second offensive was driving Auchinleck back to Alamein where the 8th Army finally stood firm. I joined the 3rd Tanks in time for Rommel's final attempt to get to Cairo, through the sand sea at Alam Halfa. Under the command of one of our Squadron Leaders, a very distinguished soldier, a composite force consisting of elements of ourselves and the Notts and Staffs Yeomanry, the raid was repulsed. Some eight-wheeled armoured cars did get through the sand sea, however, ineffectively. I was very lucky to have the breathing space at the depot in which to grasp the situation, so many officers went into action straight off the boat, as it were, and were killed the first day.

Cairo was wonderful, no shortages of anything, marvellous food and drink an atmosphere of feverish war gaiety, women and night clubs galore tremendously exciting after wartime Britain. All very hectic; playgrounds such as Groppis, Shepherds Hotel, the Pyramids Auberge, Ghazira Island, wine women and song with that dark threat over one's shoulder, way up the blue.

2

THE DESERT WAR – EARLY CAMPAIGNS

THE THEATRE

The Western Desert of North Africa stretching through Egypt, Libya and Tunisia, the countries concerned in the desert campaigns, is largely an area of limestone shingles with little real sandy desert except in the south, known as the sand sea, impenetrable except for camels and very special vehicles. The worst going was in the Quattara Depression which formed a natural barrier and a perfect anchor point for a defensive line. From the main ports of Alexandria and Tripoli was a 1,400 mile stretch, devoid of communication, waterless, empty, a logistical nightmare, this causing the ping-pong advances and retreats of the early campaigns, as opposing forces ran out of supplies the farther they advanced from their bases. It is worthwhile to look briefly at the histories of the countries involved and the origins of the Desert War.

EGYPT

The first records of world history were discovered in Egypt dated some 10,000 years ago, so that one may justifiably conclude that all preceding was prehistory. Most of Egypt consists of desert: the Sinai Desert a truly frightful place, barren, deserted and rocky, although the Israelis have probably succeeded in some development. I spent some time there at a delightful convalescent hospital at Al Arish, visiting

MAP OF THE THEATRE - NORTH AFRICA

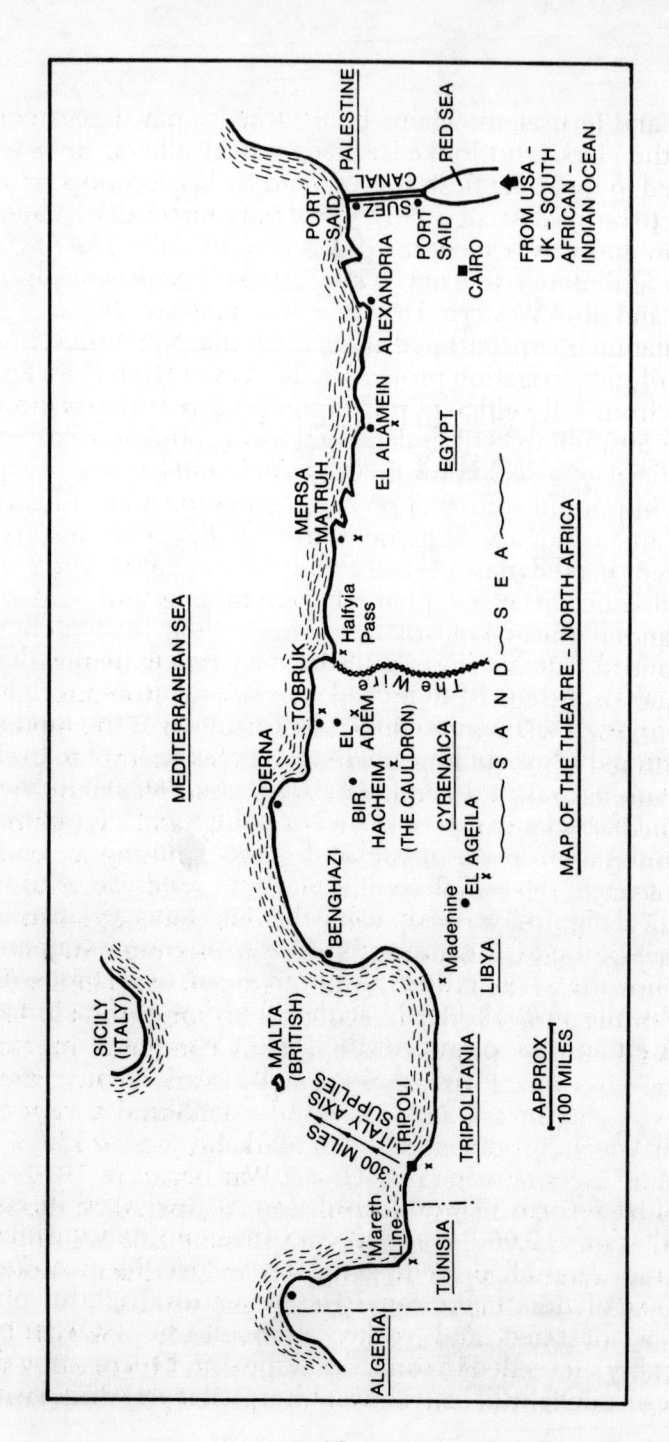

Gaza and Jerusalem, where at the Officers' pay department I met the clerk who looked after my own affairs, he was so excited to meet the flesh represented by his accounts. How I came to be in Al Arish is a mystery, I have no recall whatsoever of how and why, except hospitalisation in Cairo and vaguely of an ambulance journey. The Eastern Desert is an upland area and the Western Desert a low plateau. Most of the population is concentrated along the fertile Nile Valley, but in spite of such irrigation projects as the Aswan High Dam Egypt is far from self-sufficient to support a current population of some 50 million. Oil and natural gas production has been beneficial to the economy but tourism is undoubtedly Egypt's most important source of revenue, given the many historical and archaeological remains. Ancient Egyptian history is divided into dynasties beginning some 5,000 years BC, founded by successive pharaohs, continuing until ended by Alexander the Great of Macedon about 300 BC. On Alexander's death the rule passed to the Ptolemies, later conquered successively by the Byzantines, Romans, Arabs and the Turks up to the eighteenth century. In 1798 Napoleon established a protectorate over Egypt in his attempt to breach the gateway to the East and World conquest. The French were defeated by the British in 1801 at Aboukir and by a glorious Nelson victory at the Battle of the Nile, putting an end to Napoleon's endeavours by that route; later of course also in Russia, with Hitler following in his footsteps, equally disastrously. Egypt became a British protectorate in 1914 at the outbreak of the Great War until granted independence in 1922 under King Fuad, succeeded by his son Farouk in 1936, when Mussolini was very active with conquests in North Africa, Abyssinia, Eritrea and Libya. By treaty Britain retained rights in the Suez Canal zone and established a very élite force, which produced some remarkably fine soldiers, an absolute blessing when the Desert War began in 1940. The postwar period is I am sure familiar to all, including the 1956 fiasco, with hindsight it seems impossible that we and the French could behave so irresponsibly and all thanks to the US Navy 6th Fleet which compelled an end to it.

A friend, Wing-Commander in the RAF, took part in a bombing raid aimed at Heliopolis airbase; Heliopolis a very pleasant suburb of Cairo. As an experienced pathfinder he led the squadron of Valiant bombers which had been prepared for the operation at Akrotiri, Sovereign Base area in Cyprus. Over the target he reached for the bomb release switch, no switch! The squadron returned with the bombs; the Armourer explained, 'Sir, we had no bomb switches so I fitted windscreen wiper knobs!'

I passed through Egypt in 1949 and took a taxi out to Alamein where much military debris remained, there was a tank graveyard and a memorial to the 44th Infantry Division, wiped out in the battle. Again in 1967, Alexandria – Cairo, en route from Tripoli to Amman, we lost all our luggage at Cairo airport, fortunately insured.

LIBYA

Consists chiefly of desert with a narrow coastal plain rising to the Tibesti Mountains in the south. Until 1963 and Colonel Gadaffi, it was divided into three provinces, Cyrenaica, Tripolitania and the Fezzan. The population mainly Berbers and Arabs with very noticeable differences in the people of the three provinces. As a major oil producer Libya, previous economic activities, agriculture and livestock farming are relatively unimportant. The area was included in the Roman Empire up to domination by the Turks. In 1912 it was annexed by Italy, who were reputed to be very brutal towards the tribesmen, especially the Sennussi, the ruling tribe, who provided the first King, Mohammed Idris. It is recorded that the Italians dropped dissident tribes from aircraft without the benefit of parachutes, as a warning to other rebels. I am reminded of being on a transport Dakota, loaded with baa-ing sheep and goats, dropping them over the Bengal-Bangladesh border as rations for the Indian soldiers; theoretically, they had to be alive when prepared for consumption. King Idris was a charming old man who I often saw around the Tobruk area, when working there in the 60s.

The Queen's doctor came to operate on King Idris, alcohol was absolutely forbidden in the Palace and the doctor supplied himself from pocket miniatures. At this time the Germans built a magnificent mausoleum at Tobruk to house their war dead, very sombre and Wagnerian. The officer in charge of collecting the remains, son of a famous Field Marshal, was apprehended on his way home after the operation was complete, found to be in possession of large quantities of rings, watches and jewellery. The Free French cemetery was badly neglected but was cleared up when I informed their Consulate in Benghazi. The Free French Brigade had many casualties at Bir Hakim, surrounded by Rommel's Afrika Corps, during the advance to Alamein. Our wonderful regimental doctor managed to get into the French Box to tend the wounded; he was known as Bir Hakim afterwards, Hakim is the Arabic word for doctor. The doctor, who I last saw in 1944 in Normandy, was a truly remarkable man and saved many lives, he nicknamed me 'soldier'.

A strange animal is to be found I believe only in Libya, the Uaddan, pronounced Waddan, goat-like, but larger, huge hooves, policeman's size twelve boots, and a beard so long that it treads on it; probably only exists in the Tripoli Zoo.

The Libyans got along very well with the Italians after the initial occupation, they settled down and acquired in many ways an Italian mode of life. My experience has indicated that the French also leave their particular atmosphere in their ex-Colonies. The British bequeath a system of mainly local government, Public Works, District Officials, Railways administration, Hospitals and Schools etc., very apparent in India and Pakistan and ex-West African Colonies. To exploit the rewards of their oil riches the Libyans employed many Mediterranean people, besides Italians, mainly Greeks, Turks, Maltese, Tunisians, Egyptians etc. The Libyans themselves taking it easy.

Whilst working in Iraq in the fifties I came upon the whereabouts of quite a lot of the military hardware picked up in the Libyan Desert. Nomadic Bedouins passed frequently on their migrations following the grazing, travelling up the 1,500 mile Queen of Sheba's road into Nejaf, where I was building roads. Under their jellabiyas, voluminous cloaks, the men were veritable arsenals, rifles, sub-machine pistols, grenades, criss-crossed with bandoliers of ammunition. I saw several of the small calibre Italian rifles, probably six millimetre, with folding back bayonets, nice little toys. On one occasion a caravan camped for the night nearby, there were shots and in the morning four very dead Iraqis who were attempting to steal from the Bedu flocks.

With a population in Egypt of teeming poverty-stricken people and just over a million Libyans, Mussolini had a formidable barbed wire barrier erected on the Cyrenaica border, from the coast down to the sand sea, some forty miles, to control immigration, it did not stop the Bedus. Crossing the wire was synonymous with crossing the line in the South Atlantic.

TUNISIA

More fertile than Libya, some desert in the south rising to uplands in the north. Arab population and some Berbers; agricultural economy, some tourism, large phosphate deposits which together with other mining is the main source of revenue; little oil. Absorbed into the Roman Empire it was then known as the granary of Rome. In 1883 Tunisia became a French Protectorate, gaining independence in 1956. Population around seven million. In recent years I employed Tunisian workmen in Libya on building projects, very willing workers, easy to manage; I had the misfortune to be responsible for cutting off one poor labourer's hand. He never forgave me but subsequently I did look after him. The French constructed a defence line at Mareth, based in concept on the Maginot Line. It also did not work; although the 8th Army did attack frontally, in fact, as the Germans did at the Maginot Line, our main force simply went round it, through the southern desert region.

ABYSSINIA, NOW ETHIOPIA

With Somalia forms the Horn of Africa, on the Red Sea, deserts and mountains. The population of some thirty million, consists of Galla and Amhara and other ethnic groups; one tribe, Falashas, practising the Jewish faith, were secretly air-lifted to Israel in 1985, one heard that they were not very happy. Ethiopia is eternally famine-ridden, relief is often interrupted by internal strife by Eritrean secessionists.

Amharic, the official language is one of the oldest known,

English and Italian are also widely used. The Emperor, Haile Selassie, fled to England when the Italians invaded in 1936. Returning in 1941 when the British liberated Ethiopia, he was deposed in 1974. With Mengistu as President the country became Marxist-Leninist, with Cuban troops used to suppress the liberation movement by the province of Eritrea. We have a very good friend, a charming lady, Tsegue, related to the Royal Family, now married to a German engineer and living in Switzerland, educated at the Sorbonne and very cosmopolitan. A neighbour of ours in Cyprus made a lifelong study of Amharic. Many Italians remained in the area, as they did in Libya; I employed an Italian engineer on a project in Benghazi who previously had worked on the American Early Warning Radar Station at Asmara.

THE EARLY CAMPAIGNS

A J P Taylor in his *The Origins of the Second World War* points out that following the Great War much was written historically, due to the more than adequate available material.

> In the Second World War some leaders died during the war; some were killed at the end; others too proud or too cautious to write.

It appears to be true that little was recorded, I can find nothing about the Abyssinian affair nor indeed the Desert Campaigns generally.

THE ALLIED DEFENSIVE. General O'Connor
December 1940 to February 1941.
Sidi Barrani – El Agheila

When France fell in June 1940 the Italians came into the War alongside the Germans, having obviously considered the direction events were taking. A concentration of forces gathered at the Wire and the Italians under Marshal Graziani attempted an invasion of Egypt which O'Connor repulsed. The ensuing British offensive rapidly pushed the Italians back to Benghazi, when logistics took over and a halt was enforced to build up resources. O'Connor's brilliant use of tanks overwhelmed the Marshal and secured vast booty in Tobruk and Derna. The tanks employed at this time were the British Crusader, the American Stuart (which we called the Honey), named after the dashing cavalry commander of the American Civil War. The Italians had the M13. None of them particularly exceptional, the Italian tank was slower, which was a great disadvantage in manoeuvre and obviously vulnerable in retreat. The Crusader, a very 'pretty' tank, elegant lines, low silhouette, ideal for reconnaissance and skirmishing, but mechanically unsound and very thirsty where water was a serious problem, the engine being water-cooled.

M-13 ITALY 1940

A light recce tank. Inferior to our tanks. No personal experience with this tank. Said to have had poor performance Weight 14 tons. Speed 20mph Armour 1 ins. 1 x 47mm Gun. 3 machine guns.

We, however, had a Crusader squadron until the end of the Middle East War, very successfully commanded by superb officers and NCOs, they had to be good in their role in order to survive.

In February 1941 O'Connor was ordered to send substantial forces to Greece thereby leaving insufficient forces to advance to Tripoli. Meanwhile Rommel was landing at Tripoli unbeknown to the British.

GREECE

In 1940 the Italians attacked Greece and were repelled. However, in 1941 the Germans advanced into the Balkans when a British force was sent to oppose them. My regiment was there; they wore out their tank tracks on Mount Olympus and hurriedly left from Pireaus back to Alexandria. Many of the 3rd Tanks were captured, to return in 1945, a long imprisonment.

ABYSSINIA

In 1941 a British force went to chase out the Italians, successfully securing the Italian Naval Base at Massawa on the Red Sea. In a few weeks it was all over, the Italians alone were very poor soldiers, probably as they were not defending their homeland. A cousin of mine was sent with a British force in 1917 to stiffen up the Italians fighting the Austrians, (shades of D'Annunzio and Hemmingway's *Farewell to Arms;*) my cousin said the Italians then fought very well. I have found nothing written about this campaign, only stories from a major of the Royal Horse Artillery and Johnny. Johnny went to Abyssinia with a Highland regiment and subsequently, under an Army Council instruction inviting transfer of officers to the Armoured Corps, applied and joined the 3rd R. Tanks; he was in the élite Crusader squadron. We spent a convalescence leave together in Cairo, absolutely disastrous, irresponsible behaviour, wine, women and brawling, certainly not quite sane. Leaving by train from Cairo Main Railway Station I fired my liberated Luger pistol at the glass roof in sheer drunken exuberance; the Military Police just turned their backs, after all, one was going back, what more could happen? This particular journey was by train to Tobruk and then transport; once I travelled from Alexandria to Tobruk by a small passenger ship manned by the Royal Navy; we docked at Tobruk and disembarked hurriedly under a hail of bombs. Johnny was an exceeding handsome, attractive man, the ladies would literally lie down in his path. We were together once in England travelling as an advance party to a tank gunnery range, stopping at a country pub with an attractive barmaid, when we finished our drinks he said wait outside for me, he read the signs correctly and pleasured the lass. He was posted away before the Normandy invasion. On this 'trip' to Cairo I lugged with me a Panzer Grenadier regiment's field cash box, (loot I suppose) which I hid under my hospital locker. Italian lira, which a friend changed for me, as I recollect, some Egyptian £40. Alas my pocket was very expertly picked on my first night out, this from a buttoned tunic pocket with presstuds at each corner, never felt a thing until too late. When I did find it gone, I went berserk in the crowded street, lashing out right and left, until pulled away by a kindly Medical Officer of the 51st Highland Division, who took me to his room in Shepherd's Hotel. Another incident which impressed me greatly and I often remember the occasion when, in a bar, a South African service girl came to our table and gave me a beautiful rosary, saying, 'I can see you are going up the desert; take this with you, it will keep you safe.' I am not a Catholic but the gesture was very appreciated. Some years later I gave it to a young RC girl on her twenty-first birthday with the story.

ROMMEL'S OFFENSIVE. Benghazi to Halfaya (known, of course, as Hell Fire), Pass. March – May 1941.

Rommel's arrival on the scene caught a very much weakened O'Connor off guard, so rapidly did the unexpected Afrika Korps show up at El Agneila. The British armour was virtually destroyed and the infantry, un-motorised, could only scramble back to beyond Tobruk and up to the famous wire. Any delaying action was entirely by the artillery often firing at tanks over open sights. This was France all over again, *Blitzkrieg,* so successfully used in 1939 against Poland, tanks, air and artillery in coordinated unison. General O'Connor was captured at Beda Fomm approaching the Jebel Akdar, the Green Mountain, together with most of his staff, one I believe Carton de Wiatt, a one-eyed, one-armed soldier, also an old friend of mine with the Royal Horse Artillery, Richard. Captured officers were immediately taken by submarine to Italy in order to lessen their chances of escape. O'Connor and others escaped from Italy sometime in 1943, as did my friend

Richard. The latter crossed into Switzerland where he remained until the end of the war. In the spring of 1944, stationed in Yorkshire, I was ordered to take a Sherman tank to Fylingdale Moors Gunnery Range to await our then Corps Commander, the same General O'Connor. He duly arrived in his escorted staff car, red-banded cap very much like the Lord Gort generals I met on a railway line in France. Without a word he climbed into the turret and said, 'Shoot!' Now this was strange as the British say Fire and the Americans, Shoot, as I knew from having an American Sergeant in my crew for training. The General, by the way, was to see what the then modern tank could achieve with its weapons, mainly the 75mm gun with armour piercing, high explosive and smoke shells, .30 Browning machine guns and one .50 for anti-aircraft fire; the Brownings had a pestilential device called 'headspace' which caused endless problems. The 75 was a beautiful piece of artillery especially using high explosive ammunition. So we fired armour piercing projectiles at canvas targets representing tanks, at some 1,000 yards. This is relatively easy when stationary, but not very effective on the move.

The Tank Commander tells the gunner on the inter-com, 'Enemy tank, 800 yards (estimated), traverse right (or left), on, Fire!' The Tank Commander has sighting vanes corresponding to the line of the gun and the gunner a small telescope with, in this case, inadequate magnification of only one and a half times and cross hairs, integrated with the gun at normally 1,000 yards. I never experienced firing on the move except in exercises, although the Sherman did have a gun stabiliser for keeping the gun levelled at the target when moving. Hull down cover was sought whenever possible. Sometimes we machine-gunned the escaping crews, not very sporting, but it did happen in war. I then asked the General what he would like to be shelled, there were no targets for high-explosive. He pointed to the range limiting corrugated-iron board, a very large construction, at about 3,000 yards. Told what it was he simply said, 'Shoot it!' Then the right-hand limiting board! Finally a flock of sheep, clearly seen through binoculars, the bodies being flung into the air by the explosives. The General left without a word, seemingly unimpressed with the H E performance; this also happened when demonstrating for another general; they cannot understand the apparent waste of shells due to the necessity to bracket the target. Without a range-finder, usually inaccurate anyway, or an accurate map which in practice would be unlikely to show the object, estimating the distance is a matter of guesswork and experience. Hopefully the first shells fall short and can be clearly observed. The Commander then decides how many turns of the elevating wheel will cause the next shell to bracket the target, and so on, halving the elevation or depression until the target is hit; once on, the drill is gunfire until destruction has occurred. The creep up to the target or back to the target is hopeless.

Today's equipment is certainly very different, then tank gunnery was more instinctive, rather like pointing a pistol. The Artillery problem was similar, firing ranging shots observed and corrected by a forward observation officer, initially programmed from maps, bearing and distance, usually having time for preparation. I have seen Field Artillery fire over open sights, as we did, and once even still attached to their limbers. When I returned from the range, the Colonel was very angry and put me on to the Brigade Major to whom the damages had been reported; I simply referred him to the General.

I met up with Richard many times since the war. We were in Iraq with the same Civil Engineering contractor and at one time shared a house together in Baghdad whose owner lived in the next house. It was an amusing period with the landlady looking after us, a cunning one too. We suspected she was hooked up to our electricity and water, so one night switched off at the mains. She appeared later to enquire what had happened and we said we liked sitting in the dark! She received the message. I was in charge of the first section of the Baghdad-Kut-al-Amara road construction and one evening getting into my Land Rover there came a loud bleating from the back, a young lamb, koosi, a great delicacy.

Our woman said, 'I will cook it for you, I know how!' We invited guests, came the cooked lamb which I proceeded to carve, ghastly smell, she had left the entrails inside. Bread and cheese for dinner. She had a gormless daughter and I persuaded her that Richard, unmarried, was interested. The girl would appear and sit reading the Bible to him!

'Richard, why does that bloody girl keep coming in here?' Poor chap blew himself up on a kerosene drip device we had for heating bath water, not badly, lost most of his hair and moustache and got very drunk to recover and crying out for a woman to sympathize with him. Not difficult in Baghdad where at the time prostitutes were plentiful, even schoolgirls who wanted pocket money, but had to preserve their virginity for marriage, so unbelievably practised sodomy.

Getting further away from the desert but to carry on with Richard, who left Iraq to join the Suez contractors in Egypt, a consortium of British Civil Engineering contractors responsible for the Suez Canal maintenance. Poor Richard was 'captured' in the 1956 miserable affair and imprisoned in a school building in Cairo which he said was far worse than his wartime experiences in Italy, the school being frequently attacked by angry mobs.

I left our joint house for a delightful garden house in the Alwiyah district (Bait al Bustan). I was so impressed that I made a sketch plan intended for future building for myself. The main house was lived in by a Jewish family, very nice people. There were at the time many Jews in Iraq, particularly the profitable date export business. There were two young daughters, old enough, who used to exercise in the garden every morning, just when I was shaving; a pleasant start to the day. I went off to Kurdistan to construct a military airfield. On leave in England in the 60s, my wife and I were climbing over Snowdon, up the Horseshoe Pass, where we left the car, over the peak and down the Beddgelert face, a very rough, hard scramble. We arrived in Beddgelert very tired and thirsty but with no money! Going to the inn where my wife, a local girl, knew the publican, there sitting in the bar was Richard, also on holiday. We had a good holiday together. Going to the head office in London en route to somewhere, I saw Richard who was then working there. 'How can you stand this life?' I said. He looked thoughtfully out at the grimy atmosphere and the next I heard from him was of his retirement to a sunny place. We correspond at Christmas! So back to the war.

AUCHINLECK'S (The Auk) OFFENSIVE. November and December 1941, to Al Agheila

Rommel's problem, as was all other commanders', was the impossible logistical situation when after some thousand miles of desert any offensive ran out of steam when the opposing side could recover and send the ball back. So the Auk did very well, but when again fully extended, Rommel hit back. The British tank crews suffered from a feeling of inadequacy due to the superiority of the German weapons, better guns, thicker armour and the frightful 88mm anti-tank, anti-aircraft gun. Also Rommel became a legendary figure of invincible tactical ability.

ROMMEL'S SECOND OFFENSIVE TO ALAMEIN. January to July 1942

A frightful time for the 8th Army, savage battles at Tobruk, Knightsbridge the Cauldron and Sidi Rezegh, culminating in a stand at Alamein, Rommel again extended and the British only a few miles from their bases. Alamein one of the few defensive lines, sea at one and impenetrable sand forty miles to the south, practically continuous ridges, giving adequate protective shelter.

ALAM HALFYA

In September 1942 Rommel tried a break-through on the edge of the Quattara Depression, the sand sea, but was roundly defeated by a composite group led by our very experienced Crusader Squadron Leader. As our regimental song-writer wrote:

> You remember in September when we battered Jerry's flanks,
> The Notts ran out of petrol and the Staffs ran out of tanks,
> For the Grants they shot the Cruisers and Jerry shot the Grants

> But the best of what was left of them 'Crisp' column
> got its chance,
> As they swanned around Himamet learned to see
> and not be seen,
> A Tank Corps crew far up the blue a' wearing of the
> Green.

LOST IN THE DESERT

In late September we had a full Brigade exercise to the far south of the line towards the sand sea. We had some very useful firing with those land-battleships, the Grants, a great improvement to previous tanks, but very cumbersome and too many weapons for proper commander's control. The exercise over, on the way back my tank broke down. The Grants had an air-cooled Pratt and Whitney, radial, aircraft engine, very powerful and noisy. When starting after a long halt it was necessary to turn the engine over by hand to clear the oil from the lower cylinder before using the self-starter. My driver did not on this occasion and a connecting rod broke and smashed the bottom cylinder. So, waving goodbye, the rest of my troop and the squadron ploughed on through the sand and home. Well there we were, seven bodies with a dud tank, very little water and miles of sand. I once saw a film of a similar situation except food was the problem and they shot and ate one soldier! Seven men are rather many for a tank, but the Grant had two main guns which accounted for the extra two or three in the crew. The tank commander, if an officer, had a troop of three tanks, but otherwise a sergeant or corporal; a wireless operator/leader; driver and co-driver, two gunners; a loader for the main armament a short barrelled 75mm. The disadvantage was that the 75mm was mounted in a sponson with a limited traverse, which could amount to moving the tank to get on target, as compared with a 360 degree traverse. A modern Swedish tank has a fixed gun necessitating the whole vehicle to be swung to aim the gun. The temperature at midday was always around forty degrees Centigrade. We were accustomed to using very little water, about two pints each per day, our water bottles were full and we had a few two-gallon tins, (in normal circumstances the design consideration is about 120 gallons per day per person). Unlike those cannibals in the film, food was no problem, always bully beef, biscuits, tea, condensed milk and sugar.

We expected to be picked up fairly quickly. Our radio, whose maximum range was twenty miles, proved useless. On the fourth day I decided to set off nothwards. So, with my Corporal Gunner, a very resourceful Irishman, off we went, I carrying the most precious item, a water bottle, and he his revolver. The first day's march – nothing. On the second day crossing a vast plain we saw a vehicle moving some distance away; I told the Corporal to fire his revolver, no explosion, it was solidly jammed with sand. This was enormous luck because by now we could identify the vehicle as a six-wheeled armoured car, therefore German, as we only had four-wheeled cars. The next day we found an abandoned three ton lorry, of all things a cook's truck! It contained water and food galore. I decided to back-track to the tank carrying as much water as possible, the return being quicker than the outward trek. The Grant was still there, no recovery had occurred. It was now obvious that we had been forgotten. We, of course, were accustomed to living together continuously, only alone when going a short way off for the toilet, always with a shovel. Discipline was excellent, the Tank Commander had to be respected by the crew and orders always unquestioned (even if, as must be, sometimes wrong ones). The desert was healthy and clean except when fouled by concentrations of troops; flies appeared out of nowhere, in great swarms, it was necessary to wave them away before putting food to mouth. Except for sleep, and tank maintenance, we had a lot of spare time. With nothing else to do, I became quite good at sewing etc. For books I carried Tolstoy's *War and Peace;* Fitzgerald's translation of *The Rubaiyat of Omar Khayyam;* Dostoevesky's *Crime and Punishment;* and *A Dictionary of Science* by E B Uvarov, which I still have, a remarkably fine book containing most of the scientific information needed in everyday life. Although not allowed we could pick up the German Forces radio programmes, excellent music and always 'Lili Marlene'.

The absence of sex was no problem, what the eye does not see, etc. There were three transvestites who appeared once at an impromptu concert dressed in rather nice gowns, carried in their packs. Not necessarily homosexuals I suppose. One young officer in the squadron made a 'pass' at me on several occasions, I thought it a huge joke, nothing to be angry about. I last saw him in Normandy outside Caen after a very severe engagement with an SS Panzer Division ex-the Russian front, in which we had many casualties. Nightfall, raining hard, heavy shelling, sitting on the edge of a convenient slit trench, me and my would-be lover!. Our Quarter Master, supreme in his job, Paddy Hehir, (then Captain, but I believe he made Major), my very valued friend for several years, sent up rum for a full complement of men, when only about half remained. I dished out as much as anyone wanted and we two sat with mugs of tea ending up as solid rum, blissfully unaware of the rain and shell bursts. I think everyone was under the influence for several days.

To digress, I recall only one serious breach of discipline when a trooper shot and killed his sergeant. Unfortunately, at the Court of Enquiry, he admitted having been trained in pistol practice, ie. never to point it at anyone and in any case check whether it is loaded. Probably it was an accident but, however, the poor fellow was sentenced to fourteen years's imprisonment.

The necessity for the ancient rules of Moses and Abraham were very apparent, pork meat absolutely taboo, even nowadays with refrigeration pigs are not slaughtered in hot weather. For us, washing the body was not possible, although one could do something with a rag and a cup of water. Without circumcision the abrasion from the trapped sand soon made the penis red raw, the only solution to wash it when urinating.

So after a day's rest I set out again with my trusty gunner, due north by instinct and my watch hands. Two or three days walking we came to what must have been the end of the Alamein Line, arrested by a patrol and ending up with the Brigade Intelligence Officer, a couple of nondescript unshaven tramps. As I well remember, it was 131 Infantry Brigade, Kings Royal Rifles. So we were sent back to the battalion which was then in the north. My Squadron Leader, sitting on a case of beer, of which he was very fond, said, 'Bill, where the hell have you been?' He thought I was at Brigade Workshops, a sad misunderstanding. The rest of my crew were picked up, but the Grant caused recovery problems and possibly remains there to this day. Soon afterwards I was sent to Alexandria with the Grants to collect a squadron of the new Shermans, just before the great battle we knew was looming.

3

THE BATTLE OF EL ALAMEIN
WESTERN DESERT. OCT – NOV 1942

Alamein is often linked with Stalingrad as being the first defeats of the Germans, the turn of the tide. The Desert campaigns were ding-dong affairs, advance and retreat over a period of some two years, the Germans joining the Italians in 1941, thereby dealing some severe blows to the British forces. Finally in 1942 the Axis advance was halted on the Alamein Line only a few miles from Cairo, where columns of smoke rose from fires consuming vital records. The advance of the

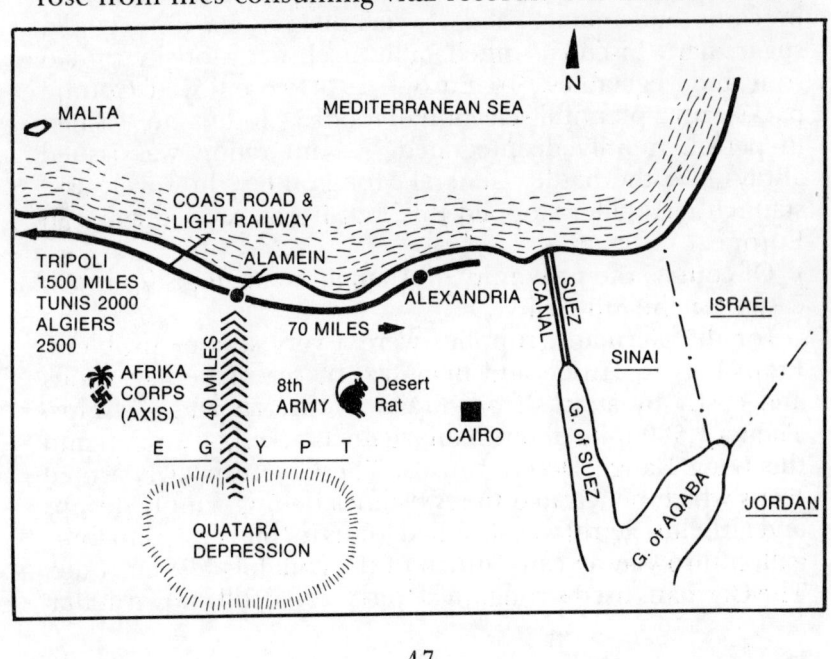

Axis forces was hindered and finally halted due to enormous logistic problems, only a short journey across the Mediterranean sea, harassed by the British naval and air forces from Malta, to Tripoli, but then some 2,000 miles of desert.

LOGISTICS

After the shorter haul Mediterranean Sea to Alexandria ex-UK (and USA) was practically halted by the Luftwaffe, except for the costly but vitally essential maintenance of Malta, the very long route via Atlantic Ocean, Cape of Good Hope, Indian Ocean, Suez became the only way to supply the 8th Army.

With the blessed help from the USA in the Atlantic, the superiority of the Royal Navy and Merchant Fleet, but at great loss, this was successful. Once arrived in Egypt, the 8th Army had to be supplied by road transport mostly by three-tonners but supplemented by excellent White and Mack trucks. Water was a great problem, all being trucked, strictly rationed to generally two pints per day, one could only wash in a little tea, precious for drinking. Food was very meagre; tea, tinned milk, sugar, hard biscuits, tinned bully beef, occasionally tinned fruit and vegetables. (In Europe 1944 we enjoyed Compo packs with a plentiful selection of foods.) Clothes etc, washed in petrol, rapidly disintegrated. A rum ration was issued always *after* the battle. General Montgomery, however, as a staunch teetotaller stopped this, but it was revived again in Europe.

Of course, the proximity of Alamein made logistics much easier for the 8th Army.

For the Germans, supplies were a very serious problem. From Italy to Tripoli and Benghazi by sea made hazardous and costly by attacks from Malta by aircraft and warships. Then a 1,500 mile desert haul, again attacked by aircraft and the Long Range Desert Patrols. These were heavily-armed Jeeps which penetrated the Axis lines raiding supply dumps and airfields. Petrol was supplied for us in 'flimsies', thin four-gallon throw-away cans, much of the contents lost en route. The Germans used strong, steel 'Jerry' cans, still known as that and used to this day.

STRATEGY – PROBABLE INTENTION OF THE AXIS

The Italians' invaded and settled in Libya (Cyrenaica, Tripolitania, Fezzan) 1911 – 1943, ruthlessly suppressing the tribes. In 1936 Eritrea and Abyssinia were also occupied.

Following the fall of France in mid-1940 the Italians joined Germany to form the Axis. Shortly afterwards the Italians attacked the British in Egypt, crossing the frontier wire (a kind of Berlin Wall), from Cryrenaica into the Western Desert. The British were there by Treaty following the defeat of the French at Aboukir and the Battle of the Nile, at the beginning of the nineteenth century. The small but well trained British force expelled the Italians and drove them back beyond Benghazi. Then the Germans appeared, the Afrika Korps under Rommel. After a series of battles 1941-42 stalemate was reached in Alamein.

Obviously having passed the gateway, Egypt, the road to India to link up with the Japanese, and to open a second front in Russia was the Germans's objective which at Alamein the 8th Army's victory negated.

OUR FORCES

Both armies were necessarily small, a few Divisions as compared with the hundreds deployed on the Russian Front, this was due to logistical problems. The 8th Army consisted basically of some three Armoured Divisions, seven Infantry Divisions (including Australian, New Zealand, South African and Indian) and support elements. The Royal Air Force consisted of Spitfire and Hurricane Fighter Squadrons and Wellington and Blenheim Bomber Squadrons. By the time of Alamein most of our forces were very experienced warriors. Following several unsuccessful campaigns the Commanding Generals were relieved and finally General Bernard Montgomery (later Field Marshal), assumed command. As events showed he was a superb commander, very austere and religious, believed to have stated that there were three things he could not tolerate: idleness, drunkenness and stupidity. In addition to the regular units there were notable extra units, Special Air Service, Long Range Desert Group, Special Boat Squadron, Commandos, Deception, etc.

THE ENEMY

When the Germans arrived in 1941, overall command was by General Rommel (later Field Marshal), again a very worthy opponent to Montgomery. The Afrika Korps was similar in composition to the 8th Army. There were three very fine Armoured Divisions, 15th Panzers, 21st Panzers, 90th Light; these names caused some trepidation to the opposing troops when known to be opposite! The Italians were inferior to the Germans and did not wholeheartedly subscribe to combat, very willing to surrender, many carried large white sheets! Their equipment in Tanks and Aircraft was poor, but they were very good Artillery men.

The 8th Army withstood the rigors of desert conditions better than the Germans who seemed to be much affected by the effects of the sun, (Nivea tins galore!) and the Italians unhygienic, where hygiene was vital. It was an offence in the 8th Army to be seen walking off for the toilet without bearing a spade to dig a hole in the sand and subsequently fill it in. Rations were about the same, we did not enjoy the German tinned meat. The desert is a clean healthy place except when static periods caused diseases such as hepatitis (jaundice), dysentery, malaria (rare) and dengue fever (saddle-back fever). Field dentistry primitive, foot pedal operated drills! Each unit had its regimental doctor, ours a truly splendid character of enormous experience.

THE RUN-UP BEFORE THE BATTLE

Due to the massive build up of the 8th Army by a tremendous logistical effort, all were aware of the impending fight. General Montgomery wisely would not commit the Army to battle until he had superior or at least equal resources. The General circulated a broadsheet message to all ranks that we intended to fight the enemy and with God's will we would win, *(Gott mit Uns!)* This was in October.

Deception and camouflage was cleverly carried out by Jasper Maskelyn* an erstwhile partner of the world-renowned magicians, Maskelyn and Devant. For about a month the Germans were kept alert and awake, the night sky glittering with their parachute flares. Amplifiers broadcast the noise of a tank regiment on the move at night. Meanwhile radio exercises passing false messages and chatter, indicated, falsely, movement or appearance of a formation. Other deceptions consisted of inflated rubber tanks, guns and transport, simulated by 'sunshade' constructions of wood and canvas. Very effective.

WEAPONS

Prior to Alamein the Germans had superiority in all weapons, particularly the all-important tanks which out-gunned and were more heavily armoured than ours. A great asset to them was the dual purpose anti-tank, anti-aircraft 88mm gun, with an extremely high velocity, some 4,000 feet per second. When a shell, happily, passed nearby, its passage was accompanied by a loud bang (sound barrier). These guns, essentially

---

* Today, 20 June 1989, my wife showed me a paragraph in her newspaper concerning Edward Maskelyn, his 150th anniversary, the father of Jasper.
'Edward Maskelyn – the world-renowned magician, inventor of the penny slot machine, hence "to spend a penny" (on all Public Toilet doors)'
My wife said, 'We have David Mure's book which includes Jasper's exploits'. In fact David M was in the Middle East but not the Western Desert, so wrote nothing of J M's activities there. The book: *Practice to Deceive* by David Mure, William Kimber – London 1977, ISBN 0 7183 0365 2.
The book mentions J M frequently and on page twelve it says: 'Information disseminated to the German Secret Service via false agents, ours, ...

Jasper Maskelyn, the greatest of magicians gave credence to these reports by fabricated invasion flotillas, tanks, aircraft etc.
In the early thirties I knew very well two charming young ladies, identical twins, Sonia and Daria, of Russian émigré parentage, Maskelyn and Devant used them for disappearing acts. Although identical twins I could tell the difference, one flirtatious and outgoing the other sweet and quiet. After two or three years they went on tour with the show.

mobile, were used as a screen in retreat or advance. My regiment evolved a tactical operation to penetrate and destroy, or force to retreat, these deadly screens. Generally lesser weapons, machine-guns, mortars, mines, artillery etc, were roughly equal, but the German MG42 9mm machine-gun was particularly unpleasant due to its extremely noisy high rate of fire. So 88s, MG42s and mortars caused the adrenalin to erupt. The advent of the Sherman tank evened things up. It became my home for several years. The British twenty-five pounder field gun was particularly good with high-explosive, semi-armour piercing and smoke. Our own gunners were the 1st Royal Horse Artillery, a troop of four guns, the famous Chestnut Troop (chestnut horses), who participated on state occasions, such as the King's birthday, with twenty-one gun salutes. Often they engaged the enemy with their guns limbered-up, ie. still attached to the towing vehicles.

OUR WEAPONS

SHERMAN MARK V (USA) 1942

General William Tecumseh Sherman USA Civil War Federal (North) General noted for strategical and tactical planning; largely responsible for the defeat of the Confederacy (South). 30 tons. 25 mph 3 inch thick armour. Magnificent 75mm gun, especially when firing high-explosive shells Three machine guns. Used from Alamein onwards. Approximately equal to Panzer MkIV – evened the odds.

GRANT MEDIUM M3 (USA) 1941

General Ulysses Grant USA Civil War 1865-65 Supreme commander Federal (North) armies. 'Grant the Butcher' later Republican President. In use before and after Alamein. A land battleship.
30 tons. 25 mph 2 inch armour. 1 x 75mm gun in sponson limited traverse. 1 x 37mm 360 degrees traverse. Four machine guns.
The 'LEE' similar. General Robert E Lee. Confederate (South) Commander, Civil War. Defeat at Gettysburg, a monumental battle, forced him to adopt a defensive role. See 'STUART'.

STUART M3 MARK I (USA) 1940

General James Ewell Brown (JEB) Stuart, Confederate Cavalry Commander. Brilliant, dashing, and unsurpassed cavalry leader. Unfortunately at Gettysburg he was off marauding, it could have changed the day if his units had been there; Lee was furious. Stuart was mortally wounded at Yellow Tavern in 1864.
12 tons. 35 mph 1 x 37mm gun. Three machine guns. 1 inch armour. Fondly known as the 'Honey'. Excellent for recce. Replaced by the Crusader.

CRUSADER CRUISER MARK I (Britain) 1939

A 'pretty' tank. Low silhouette suited to recce. Water-cooled engine disadvantage in desert 2 pdr gun a 'pea-shooter'. Two machine guns. Speed 25 mph. Armour 1-1/4 inch.

The 40 ton Churchill Infantry Tank.

Four of these appeared at Alamein leading the final breakthrough. Flat 8 cylinder petrol engine. Max. 4 inches armour. In this version another 'pea-shooter' gun. Apparently its performance in Europe was not outstanding.

PICTURE PARADE

CHURCHILL. — *One of first pictures released of Churchill tank. Speed is said to be "startling." Official caption says gun is six-pounder.*

Line ahead on Salisbury Plain. Author right top

(Courtesy of the Imperial War Museum)

55

What had just been a stormy encounter. The Sherman in Normandy 1944 still going strong; note old tracks welded on to stiffen up the frontal armour. Author leaning against anti-tank gun barrel. Note the disconsolate Germans prisoners in the ditch and the Daimler scout car behind my tank.

ENEMY WEAPONS

PZKW MARK IIIA (Germany) 1938

A good light tank, similar in role to the Stuart. Main battle tank in 1939. 15 tons. 20 mph 1 x 37mm gun. Three machine guns. 3/4 inch armour.

PZKW MARK IVE (Germany) 1941

The main battle tank in the desert. 21 tons. 25 mph. Armour 2 inches plus. 1 x 75mm gun. Two machine guns. Later a 76.2mm gun probably based on the successful Russian type.

PANTHER D (Germany) 1942

A first class weapon. Appeared briefly in North Africa. 1 x 75 or 76.2mm gun. Armour 3 inches plus. Two machine guns. 43 tons 28 mph.

The Germans had very splendid armoured cars, particularly an eight-wheeled vehicle armed with a 50 mm gun. A squadron of these did a 'right hook' round the Alamein line on the edge of the sand sea and nearly raided Cairo.

We had two notable armoured car regiments, 11th Hussars, the 'Cherry Pickers' (cherry-red dress trousers) named so as during the Penninsula War in Spain they were caught by the French, in an orchard, picking cherries. They 'saw' all and gathered very important information. The 3rd South African recce regiment were equally good. Armament was Daimler, White and Marmon Harrington armoured cars, bristling with small arms.

THE INDEPENDENT ARMOURED BRIGADE

At the time of Alamein we were a Tank Regiment, 3rd Royal Tanks, incorporated with two Yeomanry Cavalry Regiments – Militia.

The 3rd Tanks had been in the theatre since 1940, including the side-show of Greece. Consequently very able and experienced in battle and having thereby fewer casualties than most.

COMPOSITION OF THE REGIMENTAL GROUP

RHQ 4 Tanks. The then CO, Lt. Col. 'Peter' Pyman (finally Chief of the Imperial General Staff, senior Field Marshal of the British Army). To our surprise he fought the battle from the rear; made sense but we were accustomed to the CO being up front.
'A' Squadron – Crusaders. Recce.
'B' Squadron – Grants.
'C' Squadron – Shermans.
Each Squadron consisted of HQ and five Troops of three Tanks each. Major, Captain, five subalterns.
Attached troops:
Royal Artillery. The Chestnut Troop.
4 x 25 pounders
Royal Engineer detachment.

Infantry company.
Workshops detachment.
Signals.
'D' Squadron, all supplies. 'Soft' vehicles, mostly three-tonners, ferrying between Brigade dumps and the tanks. Not pleasant, refuelling and dishing out ammunition under fire!

Not least of course the Regimental Doctor and his orderlies.

The Colonel's batman, an ex undertaker, was skilled in burying the dead, (a hole in the sand) and cleaning the gruesome bits out of a repairable tank.

The officers before Alamein. CO centre front row. R. End of front and 2nd row, Medical Officer, the Doc and the Repair Section Officer.

Just before the end of the African Campaign in early 1943, my wise CO sent me to Cairo for a long gunnery course. Petrol engined tanks 'brewed up' very quickly. We could not get diesel engines as the Navy had priority.

CAIRO 1942
Photo for a new identity card, the old one having flamed. Queer eyes!

THE BATTLE 23 Oct – 4 Nov 1942

I was sent to Alexandria to collect eighteen Sherman tanks, which we had so far not seen. The joy of a night in a good hotel, a bath and a real bed, scrumptious food. On 22nd back to the Regiment with the Shermans and to learn that tomorrow was the day. A furious loading of ammunition, fuel, rations, etc, and making acquaintance with the new tank. At 21.00 on the 23rd a barrage by 800 guns each firing 1,000 rounds commenced, supplemented by aerial bombardment, almost certainly destroying the gun barrels. We were lying up some distance in front of the guns, the sky illuminated ceaselessly and the thunder of the bursting shells a continuous drumming. From memory calculated at the number of seconds between the gun flash and the receiving end x 746 yards, we were about ten miles from the bombarded area.

We moved that night to an area towards the north of the line and continued the next day, the 24th, until our jumping off position behind our minefields and the enemies', opposite our objective, a pronounced ridge, Mitteriah. There were very few recognisable locations in the desert, this ridge was one and another a lone palm tree at Tel al Aisa, which we encountered later. Some long-range shelling, few casualties, my wireless operator sitting beside me on top of the bank, pierced through his upper arm by a long splinter into his heart, the splinter was almost red hot! Also one officer, in the head, a common cause of tank commanders' casualties.

A tank cannot be properly controlled using the periscope and almost always the commander must have his head outside. Under certain circumstances the driver may need to close his hatch, in any case he is controlled by the commander. The wireless operator, gunner and second driver also have periscopes. On this particular Sherman a hydraulically controlled gun-levelling system was installed for firing on the move. Not used as it drained the batteries and was inaccurate. We always fired from a stationary position.

So we reached our jumping-off location by dusk and prepared to move into our track at nightfall. (I did not mention hitherto that the Regimental Group did not have a priest, for some unknown reason one was not wanted.) Our route was the HAT track, first through our minefield and then the enemy's, cleared of mines by very brave Engineers, mainly by prodding with bayonets, some mines were booby-trapped and the consequent explosion was fatal to the prodder.

The track was marked by white tapes and frequent lanterns. Four-gallon petrol tins with the track designation indicated by the sign, in our case a top hat, punch holed with presumably a candle light inside. Military Police were thick on the ground as guides and traffic marshals.

To digress a little, my replacement wireless operator/gun loader arrived from the 'out-of-battle' pool, a splendid fellow, London Cockney, a ladies' hairdresser in civilian life (so cut our hair), a good cook, he produced various dishes from bully beef and hard biscuits, kinds of stew, biscuited fried slices, etc. My gunner a Corporal Irishman, once before an impending attack, smoked ten cigarettes in as many minutes! Driver, a giant blond Norwegian, hence Tiny, fortunately some space in the Sherman driving compartment, so strong that he broke a track by heaving too hard on the steering, fortunately for all of us at a propitious time. The co-driver, of Jewish faith, worked the .30 Browning, a calm, placid youth, later when we arrived in a populated area he had a sale of our old clothes, etc, to the Arabs. The wireless operator, when we were one day about twenty miles ahead of the rest of the squadron, out of speech range, he exclaimed suddenly, 'Morse,' much surprised and after a moment said, 'My Goodness it is our call sign!' Morse was rarely used.

So we moved into the track, pm of the 24th, tanks line

ahead, the Crusaders leading followed by Grants and Shermans and then the rest of the Regimental Group. As extra guidance two searchlight beams were aligned on either side of the track, but of course, some distance away. The distance across both dense minefields was about ten miles including a gap between ours and theirs. Tanks crawled along hardly at a walking pace; dust awful but no wind; the moon was bright and the stars clear. The drivers could not see and had to be controlled over the inter-comm, by the Tank Commander.

Unfortunately I ran into the Major's tank in front of ours and severely damaged his carefully arranged ration boxes attached behind the engine compartment. He was not pleased!

So on slowly through the dust, white tapes, illuminated tin cans, searchlights and the occasional heavy shell. Out of the night sky fell heavy bombs, a pattern of flashes and crashes, very heavy bombs, say 2,000 lbs.

We had not heard nor seen the planes, but from observation they were coming from the east and were twin-engined Wellingtons, ours. By some unexplained phenomena all our engines stopped, except one Crusader, just as if the ignition had been switched off. The bombing continued, some mines exploding, no casualties except among the following soft vehicles. The lone Crusader commenced starting the following tank by towing, others followed and some self-started. A loss of time and a track crammed by stationary targets. Hopefully no enemy response.

Then we were out into the open just at dawn, the 25th, on a long reverse slope to Mitteryah Ridge Crest. Turning south along the ridge still line ahead, we passed a regiment of all Shermans, presumably off another track, all knocked out, burnt out, by anti-tank guns. They had sat on top of the ridge fully exposed, all wiped out for nothing. Gruesome burnt corpses hanging out from the hatches. As far as I know this was that Brigade's one and only brief appearance. We turned right into line abreast formation and slowly approached the crest, hull down, only part of the turret showing and the commander's head, observing through binoculars. This is when the ability to 'see' becomes apparent, in contrast to good sight. We had two experts, one a big-game hunter from Kenya and the other a South African Test cricketer; before the rest of us had adjusted ourselves their reports were coming over the radio of enemy locations in front. The day passed with our 75s picking out individual targets.

Some enemy shelling, causing a few casualties behind us. The enemy appeared to have pulled back somewhat, due to the barrage which continued with normal selective gunfire. One of our tanks blew up, the turret sailing high into the air, not hit we thought but due to the crew brewing up tea inside on our small, highly dangerous petrol stoves. From the prisoners coming in it was evident that Germans were opposing us, the Italian Corps were largely in reserve. A group of about 100 prisoners being escorted to the rear by one of our tanks was machine-gunned by the gunner who had lost his brother in a previous action, sad, we never saw him again. We were roughly in the centre of the line with the rest of the Brigade strung out beyond our position. In the north by the coast there was a frightful infantry/tank battle in progress. One infantry division was wiped out completely and one Tank Brigade entirely lost on a minefield, where they should not have been! Apparently little progress forwards.

At dusk we pulled back to form a laager, tanks on three sides, guns facing forwards and outwards, RHQ inside together with the soft stuff. Our infantry on guard round the perimeter. This was a standard drill when able to pull back, the enemy often took advantage of our helplessness to infiltrate infantry, where our only hope was to retire outwards, sometimes running over our and their infantry. In the laager no sleep, no cooking, no lights, refuel, repairs, replenish ammunition, etc.

On the morning of the 26th, at dawn we returned to our position of the 25th, the situation always looks different the next day, a hopeless mess has fortunately vanished in the night. Morning in the desert we always had the sun behind us and evenings in our eyes, the latter a great strain. We were ordered to attack about midday and moved forwards towards the next ridge about 1,000 yards away, the Grants up front with Shermans and Crusaders following on the flanks. Heavy artillery, mortar and anti-tank gun fire. We lost three Grants. The enemy withdrew, no tanks were seen by us only abandoned 50 mm anti-tank guns and the usual discarded impedimenta of the battle field. Some corpses, a few prisoners.

We went into laager and after a quiet watchful night, with the fight up north continuing, seen by the illuminations. The next morning we were pulled out to rest, the 27th. Our doctor offered Benzedrine tablets, to keep us awake after five sleepless days. Fortunately they worked because on the 28th we moved south almost to the end of the line, a thirty mile trek and at dusk positioned ourselves in Brigade formation, a long line, to await the morning. On the morning of the 28th we were lying on a flat plain with far distant hills in front of us. Desultory shelling by 88 mm guns with anti-tank shells, unpleasant, a few tanks brewed up. A squadron of Blenheim bombers flew overhead, eighteen planes in tight diamond formation, probably at 5,000 feet; the ground boiled in front of us with the simultaneous bursting of bombs, 'tail end Charlie' was shot down, this invariably happened, the 88 mms having by then perfected their aim. This particular squadron was South African, old friends, demoralising for the enemy. One pilot under other circumstances much later, probably saved my life. During the day we engaged various targets with 75 mm high explosive and I was lucky to hit an ammunition dump at about 6,000 yards, maximum range of the gun! Late evening the massed Brigade guns put down a barrage of smoke shells *behind* us to our surprise! However out of the smoke came lumbering four Churchill Infantry Tanks followed by a regiment of the Gordon Highlanders, line extended, bayonets gleaming, rifles at the high-port, equipment freshly blancoed and brasses polished, a fantastic sight. They passed on into the gathering dusk amid artillery and machine gun fire. We never saw them again. The Brigade advanced in arrowhead squadron formations my squadron leading. We continued all night, about thirty miles, no enemy only masses of abandoned equipment.

On the 29th-31st we continued to advance north westerly aimed at the coast road and Mersa Matruh, an erstwhile charming seaside resort much favoured by wealthy Egyptians. Some small pockets of resistance easily cleared up. Prisoners only too willing to move back to our rear. On 1 November it rained heavily! This slowed us down considerably and we failed to catch up with the retreating enemy, now on the coast road. As always with rain, the desert bloomed with millions of tiny flowers. On 2 November we arrived at a slight elevation from which we could see Mersa Matruh, some few miles distant. I was ordered forward with my troop (a not unusual occurrence for me!) across a flat plain, hopefully not mined, to cut the coast road into Mersa. A lone gun fired on us and knocked out one of my tanks. Our artillery quickly eliminated the gun and we pressed on towards the road where we could see vehicles hastening westwards. I engaged with the seventy-five and among others blew up a staff car, which my Squadron-Leader said over the radio was 'probably Rommel's', but it wasn't.

So we all moved into Mersa for a welcome halt and a few days' rest and recuperation.

Our casualties were light at Alamein due to our function of observe, hit and advance. There was no tank v tank action on the move.

During the African campaign our total turnover of personnel was 186 officers and around 2,000 other ranks out of a complement of 700 all ranks. The casualties were usually the newcomers who could not orientate sufficiently quickly to survive.

4

ON TO TUNIS

November 1942 – May 1943

THE PURSUIT

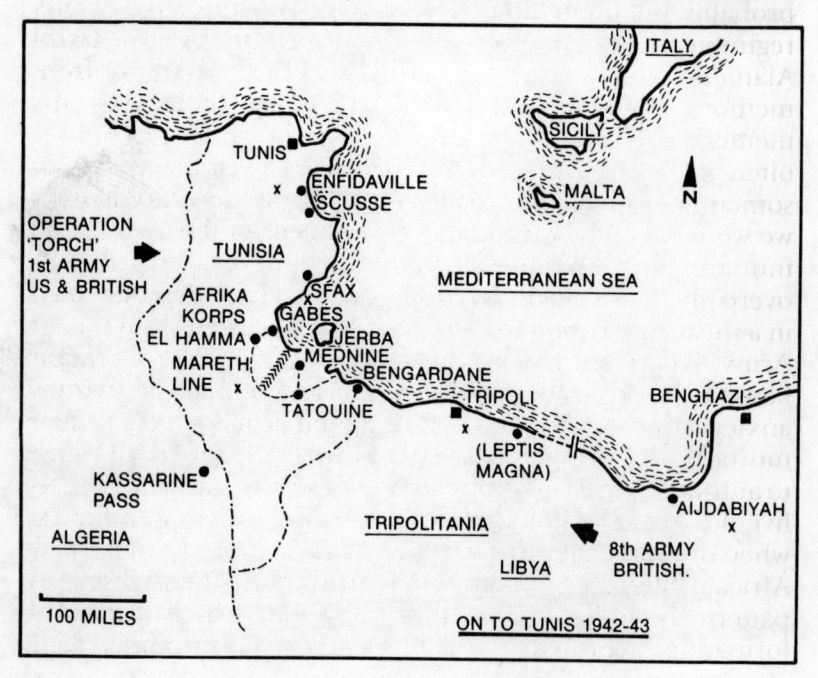

After Alamein, Montgomery was criticised for not acting more swiftly, not to have allowed Rommel to escape. With the American and British 1st Army landings in Algeria Rommel's doom was assured anyway. At the end of the Alamein battle it rained heavily for several days and with no roads the 8th Army was, at a critical time, bogged down.

The barren desert bloomed incredibly with millions of tiny variegated flowers and out came the many small things that hibernate in the summer. We were halted outside Mersa Matruh in a dreadful area, heavily contaminated by its previous occupants, Italian troops, some dead and smelly; I thought of that place as Charnel Valley; smells, dirt and flies. We moved on to Halfaya Pass dominated by Fouka Ridge, where on the approaching plain we were fired on by accurate, Italian, heavy artillery commanding from the Ridge. Our own gunners returned the fire still attached to their ammunition limbers, literally on the move. In the midst of all this a Spitfire fighter landed, out of fuel, the pilot astonished that we had 100 octane petrol and could fill his tanks. The Italians soon ceased firing and started down the pass, white flags aflying, led by an immaculately uniformed Colonel, around 6,000 men following. I acquired the Colonel's pearl-handled Baretta pistol, a very handsome toy. On our way onwards we passed a squadron of British tanks bogged down and abandoned, probably still there today. The owners were the same cavalry regiment we met in a very damaged state on the first day of Alamein. Now I never kept a diary so can only recall from memory and a map I have marked up, fortunately my memory appears to have improved with age, as I believe is often the case. Our progress trundling over the desert or sometime on the coast road was inevitably slow. Sometimes we were halted by formidable gun screens of the dreaded 88 mm anti-tank, anti-aircraft cannon. We developed a drill to overcome these deadly barriers which we later demonstrated in a theatre in Tripoli to Eisenhower and his staff from the 1st Army, who were having the same problem. The Germans hated high-explosive shelling (we seemed equally to express anxiety over the staccato MG42 Spandau machine gun and mortars), so we deluged their guns with HE from out-of-range to anti-tank shells, from our own 75s and our gunners' twenty-five pounders, at the same time creeping round their flanks, when of course they had to retire. We also had call on a South African Blenheim Bomber Squadron who specialised in pattern bombing. They flew in a very tight diamond formation at probably 10,000 feet, or less, dropping their loads simultaneously, the earth literally boiling with the concentration of explosives. The squadron tail-end-Charlie nearly always lagged behind and was an unfortunate target for the 88s who reversed their role from anti-tank to anti-aircraft. Contact with the enemy was maintained by the inimitable Long Range Desert Group, commanded by Colonel Stirling (a very gloomy day for us when we learned he was captured far behind the German lines), and the excellent armoured car regiments, famous household names operating in the true role of cavalry. Of course as with other desert campaigns there were no suitable defence lines, so it was a continuous harassed retreat.

2nd NEW ZEALAND DIVISION

Sometime around this period we joined General Fryberg's 2nd New Zealand Division as an Independent Armoured Brigade and we remained with them until the end of the Desert War. Magnificent soldiers, especially the Maoris, probably with the Gurkhas the best in the world. General Frybeig greeting us said, 'I will not ask you to do anything I would not do.' We smiled. Up to that time he had been wounded twenty-five times and had all the decorations there were! Two great gifts from the Division were fresh bread and real butter (in tins) and a very good smoking mixture for rolling your own cigarettes. A Maori Corporal named my Sherman, 'Rangatira', Chief, as I allowed him to have a look round inside. Of course the Infantry swore they would never go into a tank in action and we, equally fervently, said, 'Poor bastards, glad I am not out there!'

EL ADEM

We did not meet up with the other two regiments in the Brigade but presumably they were pursuing a similar route to ours. The Sherman squadron having a better tank than the Grants and Crusaders invariably took the lead. We by-passed Tobruk and went for El Adem airfield. The principle airfields in Libya, Tobruk – El Adem, Benghazi – Benina and Tripoli –

Castel Benito were all about twenty miles from the sea, outside naval gun range. Some enemy tanks were positioned on the airfield and after a sharp encounter and the loss of two of their tanks they retreated smartly. We established ourselves on the enemy side of the field and within hours a squadron of Spitfire fighters and one of Hurricanes, with supporting transport Dakotas landed. That night I said to my troop sergeant, 'Let's go over and see if we can scrounge a beer.' We walked over about three miles to where we could see some light and hear noises from the buildings. We went into what was obviously a mess, pilots seated round trestle tables with drink-a-plenty. They invited we two scruffy soldiers to join them. Sitting opposite us was a beautiful golden-haired, blue-eyed damsel; we were overcome! Could not take our eyes off her. Later 'she' put on a battle dress jacket, pilot officer's rank tabs and wings, a Spitfire pilot. We explained our mistake and all joined in the laughter. We left very drunk and staggered off in what we hoped was the right direction, our beautiful pilot promising to fly low over us in the morning.

We came across an abandoned Fokker Trimotor transport plane and realizing we had no chance of finding the tanks in the dark, crawled into the fuselage and slept. We woke to the noise of tank engines and there they were just moving off! We ran like hell and caught up, it would certainly have meant a court-martial for technical desertion if we had not been so lucky. Now our friend did fly over in a Victory roll and I heard later he had rolled into the ground. In the 60s I was working on two contracts at El Adem, then an important RAF station, there and the Tobruk area brought back many memories. From here on one left the coast and the mountainous Jebel Akdar region (Green Mountain), and struck out south of the Benghazi horn for the direct route to Tripoli. We were delayed by anti-tank gun screens set up by the Germans to gain time in order to halt at a possible defence line in the Adjedabyah area, which they succeeded in doing. Here I became very ill with ineffective hepatitis, or jaundice, a very unpleasant condition, at that time an epidemic in the 8th Army with many fatalities. Not very much aware of my surroundings, I vaguely remember an ambulance ride to railroad at Tobruk and train to a tented hospital at Quassasin, feeling bloody awful. The treatment then was M and B tablets and as many oranges as one could eat. Perhaps only a week in hospital and then to Lady Lampson's convalescent home on the Nile. Back to Tobruk by sea from Alexandria and thence we were invited to ferry much needed transport forward to the operational area then near to Tripoli. I drove a White heavy truck which had eighteen gear positions via normal, high and low ranges, wonderful vehicles, would go anywhere even in soft sand. So I rejoined the regiment just before entering Tripoli, January 1943.

TRIPOLI

The enemy had pulled back to around Medenine some hundred miles east of Tripoli over the Tunisian border and the 8th Army settled down to regroup in the enviable secure logistical position as the Axis forces would have enjoyed if not stopped at Alamein. Our Brigade handed over its tanks to an untried Brigade and we settled down in bivouacs. We used the Del Mehari Hotel (Racing Camel) as an officers' club; in later years I lived there for some months. Built by the Italians it was an ideal tourist hotel, a two-storey building surrounding pleasant courtyards with shops and bars, a tunnel under the coast road led to a circular dining room on the sea shore, the tunnel lined with tropical fish in glass tanks. I enjoyed my stay there. Involved in a most unfortunate incident in the bar, even now better undisclosed, but bearing in mind that one was of necessity a dangerous animal, a pilot of our friends the South African Bombers took the blame. He had wife trouble at home and the rule among them was that in such cases the culprit would be repatriated. I well remember a starchy infantry Colonel saying, 'Jolly bad show, old chap.'

We found an Italian Officer's brothel, fun for a few days until the Military Police closed it down. One unforgettable young whore screaming at *le moment critique,* 'Bastard Inglizi, you killa mi bambino.' Gallons of vino, very intoxicating when drunk like beer. Four soldiers drowned in a huge vat at Tarhuna, overcome by the fumes and falling in. Winston Churchill came and the 51st Highland Division paraded for him in their kilts flown up from Cairo. I suppose we spent most of January there until there was a flap on, the enemy were preparing for an attack at Medenine, our line being held by a single infantry regiment and a very fine one too, the 1st Rifle Brigade. Well, our tanks were handed back, *tout de suite*, and we were on the road again. In Tripoli we were subjected to frequent bombing and there was a heavy raid just as we were moving off, a very good friend, visiting me from Corps Headquarters, sitting in his jeep alongside my tank was hit and lost a leg. At the frontier town, Ben Gardane, we encountered some Arabs to whom my Jewish co-driver, flogged our few scrap items, old boots and clothing, for a magnificent sheep which we hung from the gun barrel and slaughtered. In the railway station office was a large steel safe, locked, I manoeuvred the 75 to poke through the window, opened the breech and sited the bore on to the position of the lock. An armour-piercing round almost blew off the door, inside a brass button, *Postes et Telegraphies* and an old Colt revolver with six separate revolving barrels! Tunisia's coastal strip was much more fertile than that of Libya, some agriculture evident.

MEDENINE

Our position at Medenine was on high ground, nobly held by the RBs, overlooking the enemy positions, which we could shell comfortably. We were constantly straffed by low-flying fighter aircraft and I managed to shoot one down with the .50 Browning, this particular model I had acquired from a crashed Liberator, superior to our issue, with a very high rate of fire. Our Colonel came on the air,'Who shot down that Spitfire?' No reply, but I knew it was a Messerschmitt 109. On the plain just below us we could observe a group of Sherman tanks which could not have been ours, nor the 1st Army. It turned out that they were being used by the Germans, captured at the Kasserine Pass affair. Medenine was a short-lived engagement, the next day we took part in a silent attack by a Gurkha Brigade, ie without prior artillery barrage; they moved out at around 3 am and for some while almost no shooting, presumably just silent work with the formidable Kukri. We followed at first light and met no opposition. I saw a body absolutely quartered, just like a carcass in a butcher's shop. In complete view the whole enemy force were on the move back to the safety of the Mareth Line.

THE MARETH LINE

This permanent fortified defensive barrier was built by the French similar to the Maginot Line and as it turned out just as useless. Together with the NZ Division we set off on a left hook to pass round the end of the line where it fizzled out in part mountainous and part, not so good going, sandy desert. This was then March 1943. We marched by night, my regiment leading, and were probably undetected until Foum Tatouine, some fifty miles south east from Medenine, a small fortified town occupied by Vichy French, pro-German, French Foreign Legion. As we approached I fired on and hit a tank which turned out to be a guard tower! Entering the town we met the Legion, very colourful in their well-known uniforms and *kepis* with neckcloths. We just carried on but certainly they had informed the Germans. A few days later we were at the end of the line where we met light opposition, quickly routed by our infantry. Meanwhile a frontal attack was proceeding against the Line, a friend took part in this, driving a Valentine Infantry tank, an obsolete pre-war weapon, poorly armed and armoured. He is a tall, well-built man and I am sure he was a very tight fit in the terribly cramped driving compartment. He did not enjoy the fight where they had many casualties. The night after the encounter we were halted and could see the flashes and hear the thunder of the guns, probably eight or ten inch artillery firing from concrete forts. Some were not so far away and estimating the distance by timing the flash and report in seconds and multiplying by the speed of sound 370 yds/second, I opened fire. The response was devastatingly accurate, my tank suffered a near miss and we lost our bedding etc, fastened on the back. I was deafened completely, 100 per cent, only slowly recovering my hearing after months and years, not perfect but adequate. I learnt to lip-read and still do so, it is a most infuriating condition and people are not in the least sympathetic. I grew to dislike and receive radio communications, which I could not make out and tended to dismount and receive orders face to face, sometimes with muck flying, not so funny. We now turned north-east towards Gabes on the coast, aiming at El Hamma, a gap in the high ground, good going for the tanks. Just before El Hamma we encountered heavy opposition, the enemy obviously had been alerted of our move to outflank Mareth. They were well established on a ridge some 1,000 yards from where we were obliged to take cover. The Grant Squadron was ordered to attack across the intervening valley and met with stiff opposition, losing some tanks and being obliged to retire. I well remember the Squadron Leader screaming down the radio, 'Smoke, for fuck's sake, smoke!'

We put down a barrage of seventy-five smoke shells under cover of which the Grants regained our ridge. It was our turn next and it felt rather like the Charge of the Light Brigade. We had artillery and planes pounding on the German position, but it had little effect on their resistance. Some way over one troop gave up, the officer shouting on the radio, 'I can't go on!'

We reached the forward slope and some cover. Remembering the safe door tactic at Ben Gardane, I ordered all tanks to open the breech of the 75 and sight the lip of the barrel on to the top of the ridge and when loaded with HE ordered gunfire, three rounds. The effect was incredible, the explosions hammering forward on to the reverse slope. No more from the enemy and in the morning carefully crawling up the slope we saw it was clear. So on we marched towards El Hamma and after another skirmish arrived on a wide plain where we took part in a set piece attack aimed at the Gabes Gap and the coast, and the end of the forces locked in the Mareth Line.

Tanks of the three regiments were in line abreast, my troop on the extreme left of the line. The infantry were lined up to follow and the 25 pounders to lay on a barrage. Off we went over good hard desert, little resistance when suddenly my tank hit a mine and simultaneously one of my other tanks blew up. I only lost a track, the mines were Russian wooden box type, captured and widely used by the Germans, not so damaging as the German Teller mine. The following infantry platoon passed through us over a short slope which concealed the knocked out tanks. They were cut down by heavy machine gun fire before our eyes and none survived. The rest of the company arrived with their OC who I am sure was Captain Charles Upham the double VC (it was from memory the 23rd Wellington Regiment). He was very angry at the loss of the platoon, assembled the company and himself carrying a bag of Mills grenades, went over the top. The next morning, our tracks repaired, we carried on. The slaughter among the enemy was astounding, corpses pinned into their slit trenches with bayoneted rifles. I am a firm believer in providence, divine intervention, if you like, even when one has a choice of action, it is for sure that had we not been knocked out on the minefield we would have met our doom. We picked up a number of prisoners, SS Panzer Grenadiers, nasty fellows, but by then very forlorn. Rejoining the regiment just east of Gabes, we rested for a few days and at the beginning of April pushed on along the coast road towards Sfax, a fertile coastal belt with French settlers in evidence, no contact with Rommel. Sfax was a bustling town, very green, it was springtime and there were lovely girls by the roadside, but we did not stop! From Sfax we took off across the desert en route to Sousse and Enfidaville about 100 miles, very good going rolling country, well-grassed. Having the bit between my teeth I took to pushing on alone, more or less permissible, similarly one did not need to ask permission to shoot. We ran into a pocket of Italian infantry stiffened by Germans, concealed in slit trenches among the long grass. We were hit by a Panzerfaust anti-tank projectile and grenades were thrown. I lost my cool and ordered fire from all guns and myself using the Thompson submachine-gun. The casualties were many, I suppose they had little chance to surrender. Our regimental doctor was not pleased about the amount of trouble he had attending the wounded. This earned me the nickname Manslaughter, embarrassing when used before strangers. We encountered three Mk III Panzers, they seemed to be brand new, unfortunately the gun would not bear, I could have thrown grenades at them in annoyance, but the box in the bottom of the turret was unprimed. We were halted at Enfidaville where the Axis forces had concentrated in an effort to keep Tunis open, their only line of communication with outside. I can picture the ensuing battle but recall no details except it was a pushover and we could observe the enemy streaming back towards Tunis and supposedly evacuation. The Colonel sent for me one morning and said. 'I am sending you back to Cairo!' I was absolutely shattered, what had I done wrong?

CAIRO

The Colonel explained that as the desert war was nearly over, he had to save something for the future. I was to go on a long Gunnery Course at the Depot in Cairo. It turned out to once more prove providential, my tank was destroyed the next day and the crew killed. Travel in these circumstances was a question of hitch-hiking, first on a truck to Sfax, where I boarded a large, likely looking plane said to be flying to Benghazi. It was a Flying Fortress loaned to Monty by the USAF and on board was a very stern looking general, Sir Oliver Leese, looking at me as if I were a piece of cheese. He sent over his Corporal Guardsman servant to demand who and what, but we were off the ground, too late! From Benghazi I scrounged a ride on a Lockheed Hudson bomber being ferried to India by a lone pilot who for the whole flight, sang, hummed, or whistled a popular song something like She's My Baby. I rode in the plexiglass nose under the cockpit, in the bomb aimer's position, lying stretched out; most upsetting especially when we landed at Heliopolis. Then Abbasia barracks and the flesh-pots of Cairo, dusky brown maidens, good food and drink and very enjoyable of course.

LEPTIS MAGNA

Tunis fell and the regiment pulled back to Homs, adjacent to the ruins of Roman Leptis Magna and set up a semi-permanent camp on the sea-shore. I returned in July, hitch-hiking by road this time, appointed as Regimental Gunnery Officer with plenty of firing which did my hearing little good. It was a pleasant time, good vino and lots of swimming. There were some sharks about and we found one day a half-eaten Italian sailor on the beach. Fishing with hand-grenades kept us supplied with a welcome change to bully beef. Around

November 1943 we went from Tripoli to Alexandria on a small captured German passenger ship, the *Dusseldorf*, designed for Kraft durch Freude cruises for youth organisations. We towed an MTB; the sea was rough as the Med well can be and we felt sympathy for the small boat corkscrewing on the end of the line. It took seven days to Alex. I met up with my lady nurse who was in the Naval Hospital and a good time was had by all. I had volunteered for a parachute operation into Yugoslavia, but was reported to the Colonel for disorderly conduct in a night club, involving demolishing the band. The Colonel said, 'Withdraw your application and I will squash the charges.' So we moved to Cairo for a few weeks, camped at Beni Ulid, by the Pyramids. Sleeping in a four-man tent we woke one morning, the tent gone and my sleeping-bag removed from my body, none heard anything nor woke us up! We moved back to Alexandria and embarked via the Straits of Gibraltar and Biscay, an uneventful journey except for a near mutiny over weevils in the bread. Unfortunately, a trooper who was later to be my tank driver, a militant communist, was the ring leader. In Normandy he did an awful injury to himself putting his hand into the cooling fan which chopped off all his four fingers. The doctor told us to find the fingers which could be sewn back on but without the nerves being joined. I believe such operations can now be carried out to restore complete use of the severed part. We did not know why he did this but we were under continuous mortar fire, which as I said before was unnerving even to tank crews. We steamed up the Clyde to Grenock and some home leave. I had a six-pounder ammunition box in my belongings (I still have it today), filled with an assortment of weapons and ammunition, pistols, a Berreta submachine gun, grenades etc; my mother was horrified, 'Out,' she said, and into the Thames went all! It was of course January 1944, very cold, we were issued for a time with double rations. This was at Newmarket where I went into Addenbrooke's Hospital for the removal of a piece of shrapnel from my foot. This was, as it turned out, unsuccessful and developed into a very painful hypertrophic scar. The surgeon was a well-known titled lady, the anaesthetist was a beautiful thing and I must have said something pretty much to the point when unconscious, the lady was furious and the nurses howling with laughter.

somewhere near Portsmouth, where we were locked in, no communication with the outside world. My foot was very painful and I said to our doctor Mac. Hakim, 'It must be seen to or I cannot go.' He agreed, so I suggested getting up to the Foot Hospital in King's Road, Chelsea, where I had once been treated for an Achilles' tendon injury.

He contrived to get a permit and off I went to a seemingly deserted London. The Foot Hospital doctor was surprised to see a soldier and said, 'Well, I know you are off somewhere!' It was the right thing to do, the area was packed with crystals in a plaster bandage and he said, 'When it comes off all will be better.' It came off in a wet cornfield in Normandy and my sole was smooth as a baby's bottom. On the way back I was 'adopted' by a blonde barmaid who was very kind.

5

THE INVASION OF EUROPE

June 1944

From the concentration camp we motored to Portsmouth to embark from the Hard. There she was, our Tank Landing Ship, a substantial craft on which we were to embark eighteen

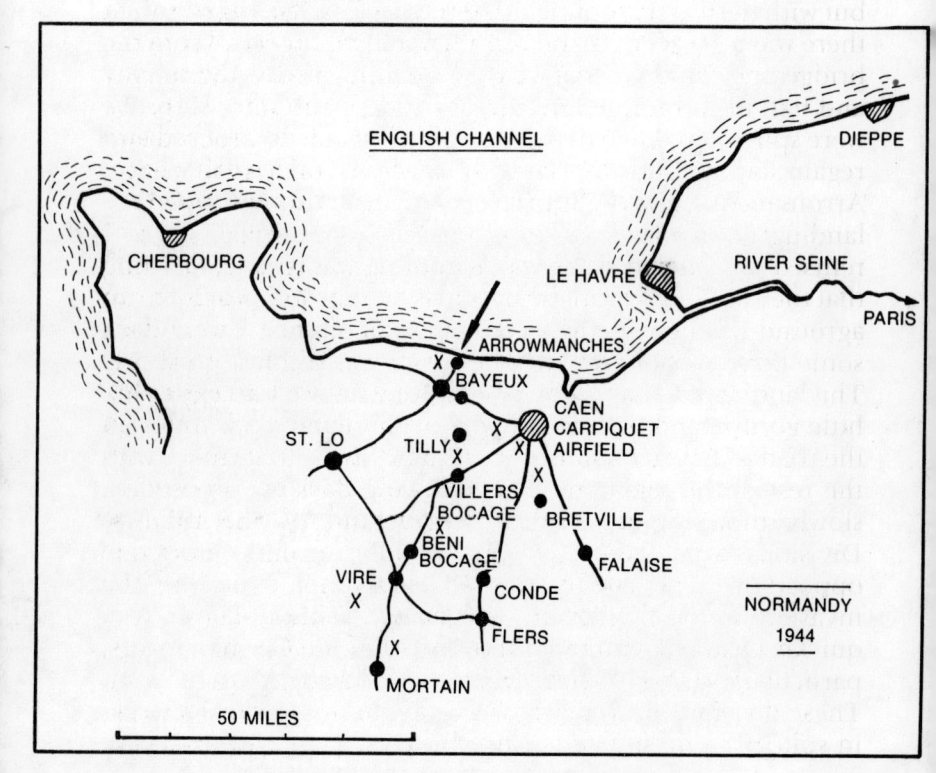

Shermans including my five Fireflys. Hitherto we had only practised on Tank Landing Craft capable of carrying three tanks.

The ship was US Navy, fresh from the Pacific area, with an all-American crew. With the Chief Officer I supervised the stowing of the tanks; there were chains secured to the deck for anchoring the tanks against movement; the Chief said the chains were unnecessary and I foolishly did not insist. We sailed into a rough sea, not very encouraging, taking up position in an enormous convoy, ships as far as one could see. The ship was very amply equipped with bunks, mess rooms, etc., we had the best food for a very long time. During the night the Chief woke me up to say that the tanks were sliding about in the hold and causing damage to the hull. He said, 'I am sorry but we have never carried tanks, only wounded men!' The hold was hell let loose. With the few men not stricken with seasickness, we set about securing our monsters, but with the waterproofing rendered useless. During the night there was a great crash and tumult of falling objects. From the bridge one could see that we were steaming across the convoy and had been rammed on the port side by another ship. We were split open down to the waterline but able to proceed and regain station. Early on Day Two we arrived off a small village, Arromanches, and the ship closed the beach and dropped the landing door, the depth of water was about seven feet so I refused to go down as the waterproofing was ruined, insisting that they land us dry on the beach. No sailor will beach or run aground willingly, being a court-martial offence. I went back some three weeks later and the vessel was still fast on shore. The landing was hardly opposed, not what we had expected, little gunfire and no mines. We moved inland a few miles on the road to Bayeux (famous for its tapestries), to form up with the rest of the regiment. The following days we proceeded, slowly mopping up packets left behind by the Infantry Divisions who advanced successfully against moderate opposition. The enemy was obviously not expecting the invasion to take place in Normandy. The situation very quickly changed with rapid movement of the German forces, particularly two SS Panzer Divisions from the Russian front. These divisions moved across Europe in the space of a week, in spite of bombing and blown bridges. They gave us a very hard time.

We bypassed Bayeux and headed for Nonant and high ground beyond, Hill 201, a Trig' point, overlooking Caen and Carpiquet Airfield. We were to get to know 201 very well, it was strongly contested, held by a strong tank force, with Tiger 88 mm gun tanks, practically invincible, and by obviously very competent infantry. On our way up I spotted four Ferdinand tracked 88 mm, self-propelled guns and engaged them at fairly close range with the 17 pounders Sabot shells, their first try-out in action. The Ferdinands were very quickly destroyed, most satisfying. The Colonel was angry, as we were supposed to be making an undetected approach, (as if one could steal up with a regiment of tanks). Near the crest of the hill all hell broke loose, most confused fighting, indescribable. We had radio contact with a Typhoon Squadron who were armed with 60 pound rockets, very formidable indeed. We carried canisters of yellow smoke, thrown in the direction of the target to guide the Typhoons. The effect was devastating and the Tigers pulled back. During this inferno a subaltern of our infantry company came to my tank and said, 'I am alone with my platoon, the rest have gone back, are you staying? What shall I do?' I reassured him and he returned to his men, dug in just in front of us. His name was Oxley-Boyle (he introduced himself almost formally!); a very gallant young officer, poor chap was killed some months after, leading a company. Night fall and as always things quietened down. I was ordered to walk forward and find out what was in front of us. Warning the nearest tanks not to shoot me up, I walked off into the night, very eerie. A red light glowed to one side, it came from a radio set in a half-track carrier, inside three dead soldiers. Further forward two figures passed by silently, obviously Germans on the same errand as myself (in fact they got among our tanks and shot two tank commanders). In front close by I could hear infantry digging in, the clink of shovels and equipment, so back I went to report.

I am not sure who started it but there was an enormous firefight with literally hundreds of machine-guns involved, the air bright with criss-crossing tracer bullets, quite useless, but it kept all on their toes. As very often happened, the impossible situation of the previous day had somewhat clarified, stabilised in an unexpected turn of events. The day was spent engaging targets with our machine-guns and high-explosive shells, lots of mortar and artillery fire from the Hun. We were relieved and moved back to Tilly, our two sister regiments mounting a set piece attack below the hill from where we had a view of a ferocious tank fight, with many casualties to our tanks. We occupied Tilly with little resistance and remained there reorganising. Back up to Hill 201 where the situation had settled down and without much trouble we were able to approach a position overlooking Carpiquet Airfield.

Our Divisional Commander, General 'Pip' Roberts, onetime Colonel of the 3rd Tanks, climbed up on my tank to have a look round. After some confused fighting against infantry and anti-tank guns we entered Caen, very ghostly and smelly, no signs of the population. We halted on flat farm land just south of the city, to prepare for a push towards Falaise in which area the Germans were gathering in great strength for what was to be their decisive stand against the Allies. I think it was referred to as the Blood Box. The attack was very similar to that we carried out behind the Mareth Line in 1943, except on a mightier scale. I saw an overlay map of the fire plan directed on a front of only a few miles wide and deep; one Heavy Regiment of 9.2 inch guns, two medium 4.5 inch and twenty-four regiments of 25 pounders, plus a 2,000 bomber raid. We were to follow behind a creeping barrage by the 25 pounders but either we were too quick or the guns short on range, because whatever happened we were among the inferno of shells. My Squadron Leader had his head blown off, blood cascading into the tank; later I inherited the tank which smelt atrociously! My tank was knocked out by an anti-tank gun. In spite of the enormous fire put down, the German resistance was still intact, the fire coming from a number of Mk V Panther tanks, well dug in, practically indestructible. Over the three days we lost all our tanks. I was sent back to our transport lines to organise a left-out-of-battle reserve of officers and men. A thankless job and quite demoralising, the only way to be involved in a war is in the firing line. Rejoining the regiment we spent a few days recovering whatever was repairable and then moved off cross country to Tilly, me in the bloody tank with the Major's crew. The Wireless Operator was killed by a stray shell burst, sitting by my side on top of the turret. A Daimler Dingo scout car, a very useful vehicle, was sent to me with half-a-dozen aerial photographs, to guide the Regiment; at a scale of 4 inches to the mile, which meant one soon ran out of the photo one was looking at. I felt absolutely lost, could not halt because behind was the whole regiment. By sheer luck I found the appointed harbour, much relieved. Tilly was no problem and was quickly cleared of enemy. We passed on this move five knocked-out Panther tanks, all from Piat hollow charge projectiles fired by some Canadian Infantry, a very valuable contribution. During our short time in Normandy we had so far liberated lots of Camembert cheese and Calvados, a surfeit from which I have never recovered, cannot abide either. The smell of dead farm animals was nauseating, peculiarly lying, bloated, on their backs with legs in the air. From Tilly we marched off along the bocage lanes, sunken roads high hedged, a slow cautious movement to Villers Bocage and thence the route to Beni Bocage. On this road a previous thrust by the 1st Tanks was ambushed by the enemy, the tanks being misinformed by some French Resistance, so-called, but obviously pro-German.

They had a bad time and had to pull back. An old friend with them, ex-3rd, lost his right arm, he was a well-known South African International cricketer. Again the slow, careful progress to Beni Bocage, a small hamlet where it so happened I was leading and halted at a cross-roads on the outskirts. Along the road came a horse and cart convoy (the Germans used horse drawn transport in rear areas), they naturally surrendered. It was a Field Cashier's unit, lots of French francs flying around! I went into an estaminet where I found two men and a woman who said the Germans had long departed in the direction of Vire. I went back to my tank just as all hell broke loose around us. We fought them off and when things quietened down I told my gunner to put an armour-piercing shell through the estaminet wall followed by an explosive shell. Afterwards I went into the wreckage, the three were dead; were they the same group who betrayed our friends of the 1st? Our approach to Vire was very strongly opposed. We were closing in on the German box. We lost some tanks fired on from a forest area where there was a substantial enemy group. An occurrence I only ever witnessed on this occasion was our Squadron Sergeant Major going out in a jeep with a red cross flag to pick up the survivors and wounded. He was not fired upon. This was very noteworthy because the days of chivalry were certainly over at this stage of the war. Aided by our own and artillery fire we passed round Vire, very easily defended country which the Germans made good use of. After a rest a short way back we moved off towards Mortain. The box was being squeezed in several directions by the Americans from the north west and the British from the north east, only the way open to Paris remained. Halted at nightfall not far from Mortain around a country crossroads with a prominent calvary, in the morning at dawn getting down from my tank I was hit by a rifle bullet and that was that.

I came to my senses in a tent with one other occupant, a Brigadier General, who had his head swathed in bandages. He was very excited and questioned me as to the situation on a certain hill his Brigade was attacking. I knew nothing but said all was going well and we were winning. He was standing, clinging on to a tent pole and suddenly dropped down dead. My next recollection was of lying in a field and seeing Monty drive by, standing up in his staff car, looking very happy. Then lying in the aisle of a DC3 Dakota, that everlasting airplane, looking up the skirt of a blonde WAAF, she was not wearing regulation knickers! Leicester Royal Infirmary and the operating table, the surgeon a very experienced doctor from the '14-'18 war, much accustomed to battle wounds. The Matron, unforgettable, very strict and a stern disciplinarian, as of course they must be. She was at the time President of the Nursing Association. One evening I escaped in my wheelchair to the nearest pub, of all bad luck the Matron caught me coming back and was very unpleasant. We were two in a room for company and psychological reasons. My roommate was a young officer who had a small shrapnel wound in the thigh; he had been captured by the Germans and operated on in a German field hospital; our doctor remarked that the operation was well done. The poor chap was very much affected by his experiences. Uncommunicative, face turned to the wall, he died. His father, an important Manchester tycoon came and asked me what had happened. I said his son appeared profoundly shocked and could not recover, probably not without very careful handling. My favourite

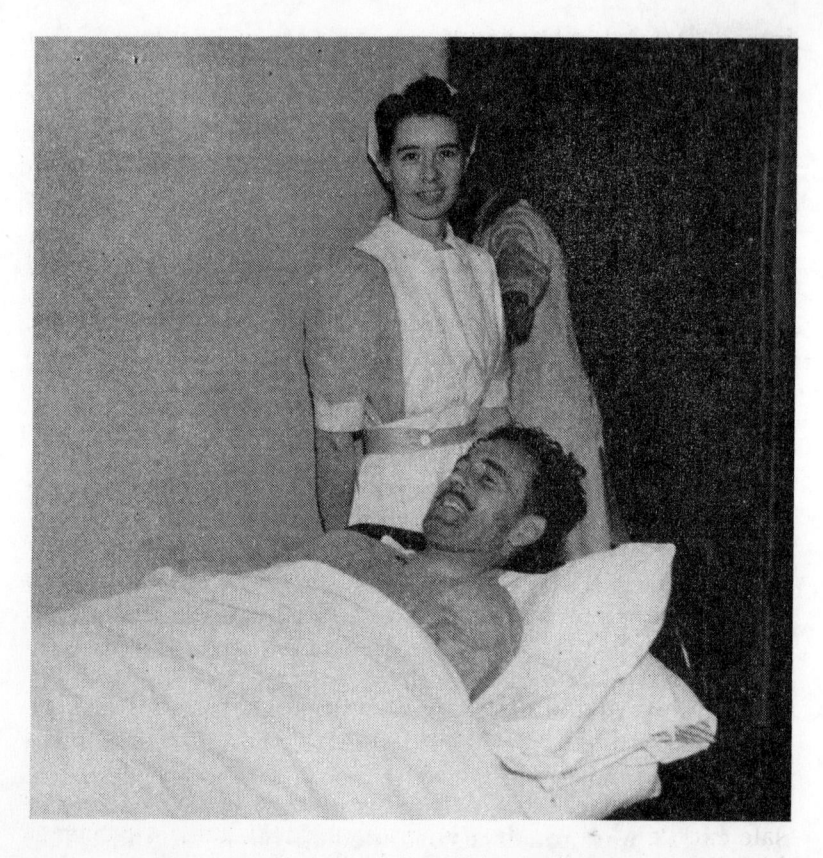

1944 Leicester Royal Infirmary 'Jessie Matthews'

nurse was very much like Jessie Matthews and accepted being called Jessie! My next companion was a cheerful infantry officer who had a bullet pass through his testicles and penis, a gruesome sight. One day being dressed by the Ward Sister he attained an erection, she never came near him again. Fortunately, his wife, a doctor, came to see him, and luckily was obviously pregnant, he was released in her care. Moved to a very pleasant convalescent home at Woodhouse Eaves, near Quorn, lovely country. On crutches I could get out to the village inn escorted by a sister, when off duty. She was the ex-wife of a famous forensic pathologist. We got along very well for two or three years, she used Claridge's Hotel and introduced me as her brother. I got to know the way back out very well. Woodhouse Eaves was a very pleasant interlude, a good bunch of convalescent officers, one from the tank regiment I joined in 1940. His hands were crushed by a collapsing turret hatch cover on a Churchill tank. I only met up with Churchills briefly at Alamein; they were reported after the war not to have been very successful.

Following a medical board, graded unfit for active service, I was posted to Catterick Camp in Yorkshire to the Royal Armoured Corps Depot in charge of the Gunnery Wing. Not bad but too few experienced permanent staff, most of whom had spent the war in comfort. I caught shingles round the waist and was wound with bandages, which one evening at a dance, unwound down my trouser's leg trailing over the floor. A terrible accident on the firing ranges; we were firing tanks and nearby the Green Howards using 2 inch mortars. A GH Corporal came running over to borrow a first-aid box, there had been an accident. I went with him and there were sixteen bodies, mostly dead or wounded! He had inserted a bomb and in error dropped another on top with a resulting dreadful explosion. He was completely unhurt. To boost morale, the CO of the Howards put on a 2 inch mortar demonstration himself and there was another fatal accident. We also had a bad one, an instructor demonstrating a German anti-tank Teller mine, which was live, jumped on it to show that it was safe except when a heavy load was applied. Blew the class to bits. A transient doctor, with whom I shared a quarter, was called out one night to what he described as a shocking affair. A soldier having intercourse with a girl, bit off her nipple. When she contracted her vagina, in the resulting struggle they killed each other, all in a churchyard. Various explosives were available in the school which I was able to play with: gun-cotton in slabs, sticks of dynamite etc, quite useful to me later on. Girls were plentiful and as it appears to happen in wartime, behaved in a liberal way, jolly good!

Early in 1945 I applied for a Medical Board and when I told the venerable doctors that I wanted upgrading to Category A, they were delighted to oblige. It took some weeks to clear up and hand over before setting out for Europe, where things were progressing on the borders of Germany. I did not achieve a posting to the 3rd Tanks but after some delay was sent to the 1st Battalion. Somehow the CO and myself instantly disliked each other, he did not want a 'spare' Captain, wanting a promotion of his own choosing. The war in Europe was nearly over after the Ardennes battle and the American crossing of the Rhine. So I was sent on the Senior Officers' Jungle Fighting Course at Aldershot, housed in a very beautiful mansion, Coombe House, belonging to the brewers, Watney, Coombe and Reid. This was an excellent course run by officers all experienced in actual fighting in Burma. It pleased me immensely that I did very well, especially as it was infantry based; tanks were used in Burma but not extensively, our 2nd Tanks were there.

Sadly the course finished 15 August 1945, the day Japan surrendered. So back to Germany and the 1st Tanks, who were in Berlin. We left from Ostend by train, crossing the Rhine over a double Bailey Bridge, a remarkable engineering feat, from the train one could see nothing of the bridge, only straight down into the river. An officer I was travelling with bemoaned the fact that his wife had lost her engagement ring, having recently broken off an engagement I had one in my pocket, returned by an ex-fiancée, which he gladly bought for £20. I enjoyed my very short stay with the 1st Tanks where I made some very good friends, one in particular 'Dodger', a common enough name in the services, like Chalky and Buster, etc. However, my home was not to be with the 1st and I was loaned to the Control Commission.

Berlin was a great experience, very exciting for the conquerors; the German girls behaved as one imagines the English ones did to the Americans, extremely hospitable. I would love to go into details, but just say that one's sex life in Germany was superb; the Black Market flourished, cigarettes being the principal currency, one often wondered whether they were actually smoked! Berlin was immensely exciting, many things happened that even after all these years are better left unsaid. Divided into British, French, American and Russian zones, but movement was unrestricted and we got along very well with our Allies. The city was mostly ruined partly by bombing but mainly by the Russian artillery bombardment which preceded the fall of Berlin and the end of the war.

Linked with a German engineer, Eichenbrenner, the

Baumeister, (District Engineer) of Charlottenburg, we first of all set about demolishing unsafe structures. The Germans were not allowed to use high-explosives so they devised a method using liquid oxygen as a low explosive. The procedure was to drill small holes at say one metre spacing near to and around the base of a building and join them with a system of wires and electric detonators. Sticks of graphite were contained in liquid oxygen canisters, rapidly placed in the holes, connected and fired. The effect was remarkable: the whole building rising sedately upwards a few feet and completely collapsing. Eichenbrenner was a fine engineer, having been responsible for the construction of some 200 airfields, He presented me with a magnificent beer stein which I still have, markings inside the lid record incidents in his life from Heidelburg onwards, including duels fought. Early days I visited a small concentration camp in Russian-occupied East Germany; horrific. What appeared to be bundles of rags were near-dead human beings. We got on well with the Russians. I had a particular friend, a very elegant French-speaking officer, a great drinking companion, all night sessions ending in oblivion. Working on a collapsed bridge site with some Royal Engineers, a Salvation Army tea-van was hijacked by some Russian soldiers; the next day it was returned with four extremely dead soldiers inside. Fraternisation came to a halt coincident with the arrival of US General Clay, it seemed to mark the beginning of what we quickly realized was the cold war, and we even used those two words. One night in the Cafe Royal in the Kurfustendam I became involved, perhaps was the instigator, in a serious fight; I am not particularly aggressive but have had the unfortunate trait of reacting violently. With an officer of the Lifeguards and two girls drinking a filthy concocted liqueur, I made a pass at the very attractive barmaid, in competition with a Russian Officer. I drew a concealed Walther 7.62 mm pistol (we had marvellous assortments of captured weapons), and he his pistol and we started firing. I shot him in the thigh, he shot my left hand, I carried on firing, hit a civilian and unfortunately an officer of the 1st Tanks. The bullet went through his hand up his forearm and out of the elbow. Shocking! Blood all over the place.

A Colonel of the Military Police arrested me and I was

handed over to the SIB Special investigation Branch, a military version of the Special Branch. Supposedly kept under close arrest, my guardian officers were quite slack and until the court-martial, I enjoyed a normal life. The charges were several, the most serious being wounding an Allied Officer, punishable by death. A KC of the Judge Advocates' Department was sent from England to defend me and after a cross examination said, 'He is not responsible for his actions, due to war service.' Witnesses at the court were the barmaid, my 'Lumpers' friend, the wounded 1st Tanks Officer, a Canadian Officer who for some reason was on my side (provocation), and others. I had a transcript of the proceedings, now unfortunately lost. Sentence was promulgated by a General (who later went to British Rail), severe reprimand and to leave Berlin forthwith, looking over his half glasses and adding disgusting behaviour! The Adjutant of the 1st Tanks forgot to carry out the expulsion and I remained in Berlin for several more months. A Professor Pulver of the Technische Hohe Schule taught me German, together with extra lessons in bed, I became fluent, the latter method being most successful and of course enjoyable. Venereal Disease was plentiful, keeping the Military Hospital busy. At one time I experienced the symptoms of gonorrhoea but it turned out to be urethritis, an irritation and discharge due to overwork. For some time I shared a small house in Grunewald with an infantry officer we called Sailor, he having been transferred as surplus in the Royal Navy, seems unlikely but did occur in 1945. In our little house living in the basement were the owners, mother and daughter, whom Sailor 'cultivated' in the Biblical sense. Although a slightly built fellow, he possessed an enormous tool; the delighted screams of the two women I will never forget and nor, I am sure, will they. With a Dutch Officer I was told to go off to look for looted Dutch paintings. He was of the Dutch aristocracy blessed with a three-barrelled surname, like Amstel-Rotter-Dam, I forget the real name. I met up with him again and his wife in Amsterdam in 1946. We were very successful and in gratitude for my help, offered me a choice of one of three paintings. I chose a portrait of a very saucy young girl, staring at me from behind my desk as I write. The Germans were near starvation, we ourselves were on very tight rations and I believe this was a period of severe shortages

1945 BERLIN. Recovered Dutch paintings, my reward

Britain. The Russians sent whole trainloads of collected goods every day to Russia, including Germans they wanted, moved with their families, goods and chattels. I was sent after a certain electronic calculator and computer expert, a rare kind, living in the Russian sector. We found him at a block of flats after asking the Concierge. He thought over our offer to take him to England and said, 'I will decide, come back tomorrow.' On the morrow, all gone! The Russians got him; we should have insisted that he left with *us* the previous day.

My expulsion order caught up and I was shunted out to the Ruhr to a mining village just outside Recklinghausen in the area of Essen. I went back to Berlin in 1958 and into East Germany, as the world now knows, very grey and grim. If I had ever had any leaning towards Communism that would have been more than sufficient to change my mind. My new job was as Camp Commandant to a Control Commission Group responsible for twenty-two coal mines in the area. Headquarters was in the mine offices and workshops. For soldiers I had the remnants of two Commandos who were being phased out, a truly splendid bunch of fighting men who were well disciplined and knew how to take care of themselves. Conditions were far better than in Berlin and we enjoyed a good life, living in the somewhat palatial, mine staff houses. The Colonel in command of that part of the Ruhr was a very charming officer, a gentleman, belonging to the Royal Norfolk Regiment. The Control Commission personnel were all civilians in uniform, specialists in coal-mining. One of their main functions was to see that the Germans did not destroy the mines and also to increase production, badly diminished by war damage to industry generally. Recklinghausen was hard work but very enjoyable, the countryside surprisingly green and attractive. My female companion Heide was a lovely girl and I also liked her parents, buxom, motherly, mother and train-driver father, who had been bombed driving a Berlin express. There was a British concentration camp outside the town which I visited a few times. It was ghastly, the skeleton-like inmates freezing in their tracks at the approach of a British Officer. The camp was started by the Americans who, when the occupied zone was divided and they moved south, handed over to us. The story goes that at the transaction they were short of some 300 bodies so they just rounded up that number of males to balance the books. The prisoners were presumably bad Nazis, but as we often said, who in Germany did not support Hitler? Very few. A chap I met had acquired a Caterpillar Bulldozer, a very expensive piece of equipment. He got this back to England and started a plant hire business, it was transported by a Tank Landing Craft. In the Mess garden we had a large pig which we decided to eat and I was to kill. On receiving the first revolver bullet, aimed at where I thought its heart to be, Mr Pig jumped up, crashed through its pen-sty, and was loose in the garden and quite cross! Four more bullets achieved nothing. The sixth and last, as we found when opening the head, had penetrated the very thick frontal bone and just nicked the brain. The effect was startling. The pig leapt on all four legs several feet up and dropped down dead. The brain was about the size of a hen's egg. We had pork for weeks. A frequent visitor to my quarters was a Major from a Highland regiment stationed in Essen who came weekends bringing his soldier servant. The kilted Major successfully courted charming, twin girls, young teenagers, who became pregnant, proudly walking together along the street displaying with pride their swollen condition.

One weekend the servant got very drunk and went down the mine, when, in the early hours of a Sunday morning, the German Police telephoned me to come and deal with the potentially dangerous situation. They were not allowed to interfere with British military themselves. As I walked along the workings he stepped back into a recess (a refuge for walkers along the mine railway), brandishing a smashed bottle, 'I'll kill you, you bastard!' He obviously did not succeed and I had him locked up in the police cell. The next morning he grovelled, 'Please don't charge me, etc.' I did nothing, let him free. There was a small hotel in the village, probably only some twenty rooms, where every week we held dances, very enjoyable they were too. A Commando was served raw rocket spirit in the hotel and consequently went blind. At the following party, I led and encouraged what turned out to be the practical destruction of the hotel. The band fled and it was comical to see the drummer with his large instrument wrapped round him. Our Military Police arrived

1947 GERMANY FLENSBURG   Self   Paddy

1947 GERMANY FLENSBURG
Col. Teddy *background*, Self and Paddy *foreground*, backs.

and when I explained what had happened turned their backs and went away. The hotel, or what remained of it, closed and we had to seek another party place. The armaments' family, Krupp's palatial house, Villa Hugel, was the HQ of the Control Commission, a very beautiful house, furnishings and paintings. From Soligen I acquired a case of seven open razors, which I still use today, all for five cigarettes! It was a good time at Recklinghausen but feeling like a change and perhaps with an eye on a permanent commission, I applied for a posting to my old regiment, 3rd Royal Tanks, then stationed at Flensburg in Schleswig Holstein, on the Danish border. The transfer came through and off I went with fondest farewells to Heide. This was in 1947.

It was good to be back and to feel once more like a soldier. Very few familiar faces remained. Paddy Hehir, Quartermaster and backbone of the Regiment was there, now in married quarters, as comforting to have around as always. A few officers and troopers I knew, but most pleasing my friend Dodger posted from the 1st Tanks. Some of the old stagers, captured in 1941 in Greece, had returned, notably the RSM and the Second-in-Command, seemingly unmarked by their long imprisonment. Apart from morning squadron duties life was devoted to sports. The day I rejoined the Colonel, Teddy Mitford, one-time Brigadier General (a splendid officer under whom I would have liked to have served during the fighting), interviewed me together with Dodger. He said, 'Bill, you have a reputation for getting into trouble, Dodger you will look after him.' And Dodger did, seeing me through several scrapes, a great back-up man. He saw me through a nasty affair with the widow of a British Naval Officer, found in her bed when I should not have been. Dodger dealt very competently with the brawl that followed.

On report to the Colonel he said, 'Go away and write em an explanation!' Well, I wrote: I felt ill and the sympathetic lady put me to bed. The Colonel smiled. We had a good stable, horses that the Germans had purchased from the British Cavalry, marked with the broad arrow. We had an ex-Dragoon, rough-riding instructor, a very interesting soldier, knew all about horses and had established a riding school. Horses just did not like me and usually behaved badly, reaching round and nipping my knee and several times standing on my foot and literally laughing! We had a fine collection of yachts in the fjord, thirty square metres and some small, very swift boats the name of which I have forgotten. Sailing was a joy and I was passed out with First Mate's rating in sail by the RN Officer in charge of the port. I had a steady girl friend, a Norwegian who had been wed to a German. She was a remarkable sex acrobat, I often wondered what that meant! The ex-POW Second-in-Command found the somewhat exacting role of PRI, President of the Regimental Institute too exhausting and so I became PRI. Under the prevailing circumstances we were being supplied by the NAAFI with all commodities, except food, the PRI role was to obtain and account financially for all such other supplies, cigarettes, drinks, locally purchased items, ie from adjacent Denmark; to oversee the various messes from officers down to ORs; to organise entertainments, sports, dances etc., all very time-consuming and instructive. I had a clever sergeant who extracted more than was due from the NAAFI. was caught out and quietly posted away, no charges, no fuss, the regiment looked after its own. Every two months there was an audit of the PRI finances, stocks, etc., involving completion of a four-page army form, setting out details of income and expenditure. I never understood how the final figures were arrived at and I suspect that neither did anyone else, but the end sum had to correspond with something in the ledgers; it was a headache. Unlike many company reports one scans there was no way to balance the accounts with those mysterious items such as contingencies, write-offs, debts, etc., which I invariably suspect. At the Vier Jahren Seits Hotel in Hamburg there was a fracas in which my Dodger flattened the manager. This time it was my turn to plead with Teddy that Dodger was attacked and defended himself against brutal odds! We went to one of those queer places found in Hamburg's Reeper Bahn, frequented by transvestites clothed in garments of the opposite sex. I interrupted a dancing pair, very attractive 'girl' the 'man' objected and laid hands on me. Dodger floored the male person who was carted off to the Ladies' toilet! What a wonderful comedy could be woven round such a scene. There were German navy sailors and marines in Flensburg, uniformed still serving, employed in mine clearing. A corporal I had known for several years, was one night severely beaten up by a group of these. Next night with the corporal's Troop Officer I went on an Afghan raid on the port area. It was highly successful. The German Police could not interfere with allied forces' personnel, especially officers. Of course it was reported and we were up before Teddy. Before he dealt with the case I said that I was to blame entirely and would forthwith resign, which I could since I had merely served on after the end of the war. In spite of the prospect of promotion and a regular commission, I had already decided that peace time soldiering was not for me. The Colonel invited Dodger and myself to his house for dinner that night, when the subject was not mentioned. By mutual agreement I stayed on for a month to hand over and after a magnificent farewell dinner caught the morning train en route to Cuxhaven then early 1948. Before leaving our MO suggested a medical board, when I was then downgraded to unfit. Instead of a pension I accepted a one-off gratuity. At Cuxhaven I met up with a Grenadier subaltern with a party, escorting the Colours to England; we had lots of relatively worthless cash, so spent a good night, staggering on to the ship, the Colours carefully carried by the Escort Sergeants. The Demob Depot and an awful civilian suit, never to be worn. I took a few weeks of my four months leave and then attacked the difficult problem of settling down in a civilian life after ten years in uniform.

6

FOLLOWING THE SUN

It proved incredibly difficult to settle into civilian life, more so than in later retirement from active employment. Employment was not easy to find but after many abortive written applications, I called at the obvious place, the Labour Exchange. They sent me to a small engineering company specializing in the design of vessels in stainless steel, mainly for the dairy, brewery and soft drinks industries. I was taken on as a design draughtsman, enjoyed very much the work and probably would have progressed to a senior position in the firm. Living with my parents in Surbiton, life in the unwelcome austerity, worse apparently than during the war, blamed probably quite rightly on the Labour government, which astonishingly ousted Churchill, egged on the overwhelming desire to get away from the greyness of life as it was, back to the unforgettable blue skies and sun. Quite remarkably Germany in 1948 was recovering from her post-war state. Lose the war, win the peace, always seems to happen. I applied for many advertised situations, always abroad, absenting myself frequently from my job, sick in bed with flu, or some such excuse. Always the same story. 'Too many like you seeking the position, sorry!'

Then what I like to think of as my old friend providence stepped in. Interviewed and rejected by an oil company of the Esso group, I was waiting for a lift in the the hall outside when a door opened and a voice said, 'Just the man we are looking for, when can you start?' Quite incredible, but within the month I was on a flying boat out of Southampton bound for Bahrain, a leisurely five days flight stopping at Sicily, Alexandria, Basra and on to Bahrain in the Persian Gulf, otherwise known as the Arabian Gulf.

My seat companion was the Personnel Manager of the Qatar Petroleum Company. On learning I was going to Bahrain he said, 'Why are you not coming to us?' I told him I had been turned down by his office. He wrote down the relevant particulars, saying, 'Well, when can you join us?'

This was, of course, not possible. I was on a three year contract.

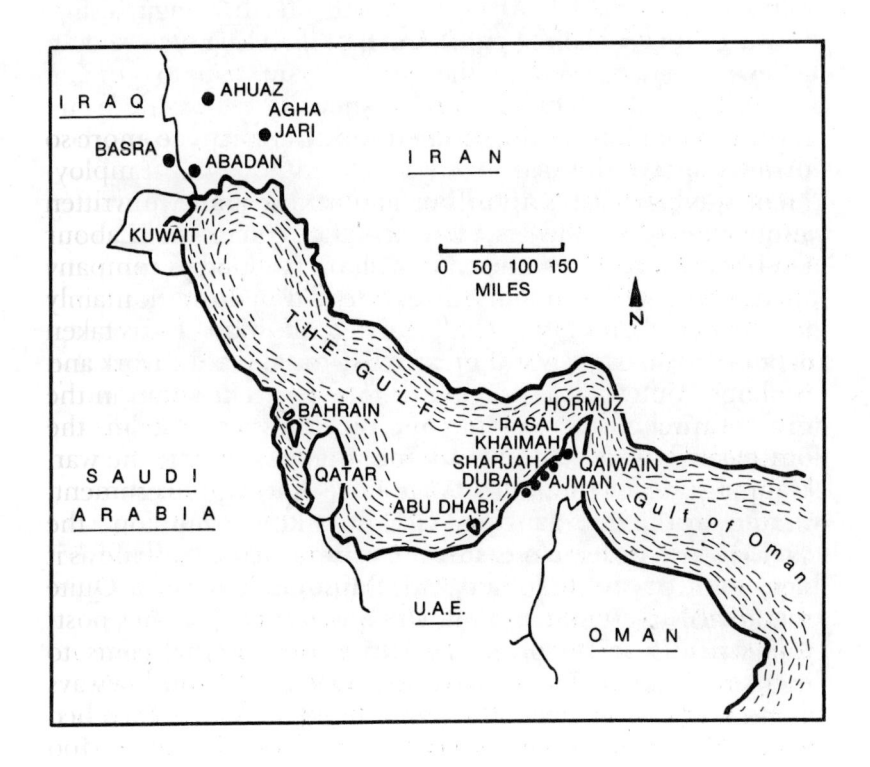

BAHRAIN

Bahrain was to me the schoolroom, American know-how, expertise and such important items as standards and standardisation, put me on the right path for the future. If willing to learn, the opportunity was there. A course in colloquial Arabic which if passed carried an additional monthly payment. I have made a practice of learning something every day; yesterday I found out about Laser, what the word stood for and how generated; why tyre pressures on a car are lower in front, a question of aerodynamics, which in fact I worked out myself. If required to do a job, have a go, likely you will succeed. Who speaks German? I do, a whole night spent struggling with highly technical German on a pamphlet describing a special pump and its function, no dictionary available! After a month in the engineering drawing office, detailing pipework, the Chief Engineer said, 'I believe you are used to the sun, I want you to go out surveying', (of which in fact I knew little except from geography, geometry, trigonometry and gunnery). So another fortuitous step forward.

The Gulf climate is appalling, extreme heat and humidity with only brief winters, but a little cooler then. Air-conditioning almost a must and with oil companies certainly provided. In other circumstances one had to do without. We had an excellent Mess Hall, very good food and cheap alcoholic drinks, (it was a great relief to take a drink in the evenings, somewhat a strain for teetotallers). The survey work was comprehensive, setting out pipelines and buildings, locating oil wells, adding to the trigonometrical survey, strapping (measuring) oil storage tanks and various vessels, marine work, tide gauging, etc., etc. Tank strapping was carried out in order to measure the volume of the tank inch by inch and fractions of an inch, absolutely vital as this established the volume of oil which was sold.

The field work involved measuring the external circumferences of the tanks at intervals, suspended from bosuns' chairs using invar steel tapes, very nerve-racking, especially when being pulled up or lowered. When I told the chain boys we were going strapping, faces would go grey! This condition is more noticeable in coloured people under stress of fear, supposedly white persons turn pale. One memorable marine job was checking the geographical location of a light marking a channel twenty-six miles from the coast. The light and platform was suspended on steel piles several metres above mean sea-level and from the platform could be seen a great variety of marine life; small fish sheltering round the piles, attacked by larger fish and finally sharks, fantastically,

1948 BAHRAIN. Setting out in the refinery

1948 BAHRAIN. The Virgins Pool

powerfully moving with the speed and force of an express train. Locating and driving the first pile for a marine railway, viewing from a boat I said to the Construction Superintendent, 'My God, the pile is floating up and down!'

'You fool, it is us and the boat going up and down, a remarkable illusion.'

Since Bahrain was a British Protectorate the Treasury in 1949 insisted that the Oil Company observed the then stringent monetary regulations. This was very noticeable in the deterioration in the quality of our imports, hitherto from America, emphasized later on when I was supervising the construction and furnishing a house for a Vice-President of the company. One exercise in the Island Survey was to link Bahrain accurately with Qatar, using an established trig station on Jebel Dukhan, the Smoky Mountain, and the refinery gas flares in Doha. In order to do this we had to lug our gear up the mountain in the heat of August; tempers frayed and I fought with one of my chain men, Hassan, rolling over on the sharp rocks. Neither won, poor Hassan died from syphilis the following year. Decca Navigator using aircraft-borne instruments, ran a check on the island trigonometrical survey, which had been principally carried out by a first-class American surveyor, from a base line some fifteen miles long which he established. The aerial survey checked in very well. I shared a Swedish prefabricated bungalow with two Australians and an English refinery chemical engineer. We had an old Buick saloon car and a Dhow, which was named *Rawa-al-Hawa, Spirit of the Wind,* great fun on our Fridays off. I had been Chief Surveyor for sometime when I was made Township Engineer for Construction and Maintenance of the oil company town at Awali. At a period of expansion very much construction was carried out in my time, 100 houses, new swimming pool, cinema, club, commissary, etc., my final effort being the planting of 10,000 trees and bushes. I was told some years later than Awali was now a green oasis.

I became involved in the so important sewage disposal problem, at that time collected into an eighteen inch diameter outfall into the sea, no treatment. One day the toilets overflowed and opening manholes along the line found the blockage; it was a French letter snagged in the pipe and inflated, acting like a stopper. One day we had prawns for lunch, some 500 were stricken by violent diarrhoea, keeping the hospital very busy. Prawns and other fish will feed on sewage and these were caught in the area of the discharge. We had a Syrian dentist who had four wives, his sewage was always in trouble with sanitary towels, they being the enemy of sewage disposal. There were only a few female employees apart from some wives, so generally it was a bachelor existence. The girls were mostly stenographers or nurses, unfortunately they took advantage of their dominant situation and behaved somewhat badly. Better none at all! In my last year I was, shall we say, 'lucky', one of the few. Not a very happy situation, many such liaisons inevitably ended up in marriages, which would not have occurred under normal circumstances. When the Vietnam War broke out I learned that my old regiment was there and volunteered to join them, as I was still on the reserve. The reply was, too many officers in your age group, sorry. We had little contact with the commercial expatriates in the capital town, Manama, on the north coast; oil companies tend to keep very aloof due to their superior importance. Near Manama was the Virgins Pool, a spring-fed pond of beautiful blue water, where we went bathing at night. The water was fresh and the source must have originated under the sea, where fishermen and pearl-divers obtained drinking water. Wooden barrels weighted with rocks and bunged with a line attachment were lowered to the sea bed, pull out the bung and the barrel filled. The pearl-divers were young men with stout chests who dived with a wooden nose clip and an apron bag to hold the oyster shells. They could stay down for as much as five minutes. It was a dead-end job, few lived more than thirty years. In the desert not far inland from the Virgins Pool we built a small crematorium, a concrete structure fired by a 900 degrees Centigrade gas burner, which I found in the Refinery, used for the distillation of oil. It was only used once in my time.

There were ladies of easy virtue to be had in the town, variously known as ---black or ---white, according to hue. Two apprehended during the month of Ramadan were tied in gunny bags and publicly beaten to death, the executioner using a palm tree branch. The airport was on Maharraq Island, joined to the mainland by a causeway, the island itself only a few feet above the sea level. Planes approached very low over the sea for several miles. One night an Air France Super Constellation carrying refugees from Dien Bien Phu, the point of final exit by the French in their Vietnam war, crashed into the sea, short of the runway, all 104 people on board died, many of them were nuns; the company photographer told me that most of the bodies were stripped of their clothing, due to the force of entry into the sea. The next night another Constellation on the same evacuation mission also crashed close to the previous one, all killed.

I was in 1951 supervising the construction of a magnificent house for a Vice-President of Esso, along the coast at Manama at Khor Khaliya, a Royal Navy anchorage. President Phillips was a very important figure in the oil business, very exacting and strict. He was a great gardener and the house was named Al Bustan, The Garden. My first job was to carry out a plane table survey of the land, locating and naming every tree, plant, bush (and probably even weeds), before construction commenced and absolutely nothing was to be harmed. The changeover to sterling was the most noticeable particularly at this time and most unfortunately in this house, when Eddie Phillips was furious with a sad procession of faulty items ex the UK. To mention a few: Venetian window blinds were all sent with widths and lengths interchanged, reversed, so that they would open horizontally! The very expensive furniture was wrapped in brown paper which firmly adhered to the wood finish. A lovely old craftsman, Jack, came out and spent two months restoring the surfaces. The fitted carpets were cut and supplied from an old drawing, although the firm had the revised details. All scrapped. Electrical appliances were mostly the wrong voltage. US standard is 110-115 volts for all domestic use.

Many other discrepancies which I have forgotten. I struck trouble with Eddie who ordered me to be fired! A Coventry Climax fire pump was to be installed in the garden. In excavating for the concrete base, roots were cut and destroyed! His Lordship nearly died from apoplexy. My boss, the Chief Engineer laughed. Finally I moved to the Refinery as Construction Engineer mainly responsible for cooperating with Bechtel, a very big construction company who were carrying out a Refinery extension. Altogether Bahrain was a marvellous experience, shaping up things to come. I went on long leave taking my lady companion for a holiday to Cyprus when of course her premium asset, shortage of females, vanished. This decided me not to return to Bahrain as I would have certainly be expected to marry the girl, who was returning and was very popular.

Home in England, looking around I spotted an advertisement in the *Evenign News* for an Engineer/Surveyor, Gold Coast. At the interview the company director had been in Bahrain and whatever; I got the job.

THE GOLD COAST (GHANA)

The air route then was by BOAC to Lisbon and there to catch a Pan Am Stratocruiser from the States, which served the West African coast and Accra where I was bound. The Stratocruiser was delayed for a couple of days so we were put into a pleasant hotel, the Flamingo. Here I met a couple of American school teachers, brother and sister; we became friends and corresponded for several years, they sending to their man-in-the-bush, from time to time interesting books. So to Accra and that overwhelming aroma, all-pervading, compounded of humid air carrying the scents of spices and above all hardwoods, mahogany and sun-dried fish, all rather like the smell of an old-fashioned, cedar-wood pencil. The project was the construction of first phase of the University of the Gold Coast, at a site on the Dadowah Road at Legon Hill some thirteen miles from Accra, comprising the Halls of Residence and services, water supply, sewage disposal, roads, etc. Legon had strong juju, witchcraft associations, involving the Royal Python a beautiful, harmless snake, but much feared by the Africans. The Gold Coast, once centre of the slave trade, was a British Colony from 1875 until Independence in 1957. When I went there in 1952, Kwame Nkrumah was in jail, subsequently he became the first president. Ghana had mainly cocoa, gold and diamonds, and timber for export, but is dogged often by crop failures. The population is around thirteen million; the Coast peoples, often mission-taught, sometimes appear more civilized, the interior, a mixture of Fulanis, Ashantis, some cannibals even, none of them troublesome, all pleasant and easy to get on with, black to coffee-coloured in hue. English is the official language, as there are so many tribal dialects. Takoradi is the main port, goods at that time were landed at Accra by large canoes, skilfully handled through the enormous offshore rollers. Once a coaster, always a coaster, a fascinating life for expatriates, in trade and commerce, government, public works and social services.

The British were excellent colonisers and when they got out, left a first-class system of government, enduring for many years after Independence. The women, known always as mammies, ran the show; industrious and good at business; the men inclined to be lazy. The old slave routes from the West Coast, to Djibouti on the Red Sea and thence to Mecca, were constantly travelled, carrying pilgrims and probably slaves, the latter still popular in Arabia. The vehicles, known as mammy wagons, were crude bus bodies locally built on a lorry chassis, frequently Bedfords, a type to be found in many countries from the Middle East through Africa and India. Always jammed with passengers, luggage and livestock on the roof, drums of water behind, painted signboards, Allah Akbar, God is all, Marry Woman – Kiss Snake (how true!), favourite ones. Most expatriates had 'wives', a very sound arrangement, they were good spouses, looked after their man, cooked, washed, etc, and were most faithful. They probably used an effective method of contraception, since one never encountered offspring from these liaisons. I was not one of these married couples, but did have a special friend who ran a bar at Labadi Beach near Accra. Labadi was a great spot for surfing, one could walk out about a mile and surfboard in at alarming speed. It was also very dangerous, many swimmers were drowned. The Atlantic rollers, travelling thousands of miles, struck the coastal cliff with great force and divided, part running down and the crest sweeping on to the shore. The object was to mount the crest as it broke; if one went a little further out it was likely to be fatal, getting into the downward surge. We lost two men, one possibly deliberate.

There were some fifty expatriates on the project, most of whom had seen military service, hand-picked, tough, very good at their jobs. We had a few deaths and the carpenter-shuttering foreman very skilfully made coffins of two inch thick, reinforced concrete. Apart from malaria, for which one took daily prophylactics, probably nivaquin in those days, there were many other unpleasant diseases. My job was to survey and make record plans, of a virgin bush area for a future University extension along some five miles of the Dodowah Road, by about one mile in depth. This involved cutting bush paths on a 100 feet grid, with existing ground levels taken at intersection points, together with recording the location of the few features such as trees.

The Project Manager, a very capable administrator and organizer, a well-known Bisley Rifle Shot, gave me dinner the night I arrived, his wife said, 'I would not go down to the bottom of the garden for a million pounds!'

Freddie said to me, 'But you are going to!' The bush, thick thorns, cactus and tough grasses was infested by all kinds of poisonous snakes, the worst and most hideous looking being the puff-adder, or perhaps the spitting cobra or mamba – not much choice. I employed a bush clearing gang of men from the interior, the chief being a cannibal, with filed-to-a-point teeth and elaborate facial cicatrices, he was much feared by the other men. I often wondered how it was possible to file the teeth, but years later having my teeth capped, there was no pain, as the nerve is central. My survey gang, chain men, mostly coast boys, ex the Church Mission Schools, were easily found, West Africans readily take to land surveying and the Gold Coast Survey Department was very active. With the bush clearers was a hunter armed with an old muzzle loading musket, primed with gunpowder and assorted nails and bits of iron, for killing snakes. However, if there were too many reptiles about my gang would all run off and leave me miserably alone in the bush!

In the evenings I would plot the days survey, monotonous but rewarding. We were housed in four man mud brick huts, very primitive, four bedrooms, a bathroom, lounge and verandah. We had a small club where some very heavy drinking was current, but they were not the kind to let it interfere with work. Two foremen one evening had a stupid bet, as to who could drink a whole bottle of whisky at one go, in the shortest time. They did, getting redder and redder in the face. The winner said, 'Cissie, let's have another bottle,' promptly falling unconscious on his back, the other walked to the bar for a bottle, but never made it, he passed out. One was partly paralysed for weeks, the other apparently unharmed. In later years I saw an army sergeant do this with a bottle of brandy and he dropped dead.

The Lisbon Airport Hotel was great fun, a long bar, favourite place when a plane was due, to see new faces. Christmas Eve 1952 was a very memorable occasion for me, standing at the bar with my back turned to them, five officers from the Gold Coast Regiment were actually talking about myself.

'Do you remember old Manslaughter? Poor chap, he was killed in Normandy.'

I turned and said, 'Good heavens, it is me you are talking about!'

We had some good times in their mess, well-known for excellent palm oil chop. That same evening I danced with and took outside, a beautiful coffee-coloured girl, educated at the Sorbonne she told me. The next day someone said, 'You lucky man, she is the Ashanti Diamond Princess!'

The survey took eight months and the Chief Civil Engineer going on leave for four months, I took over from him, added experience. I then shared a bungalow with our Quarry Master, responsible for producing the building, paving and concrete stone, one night I nearly shot Hutch! A sub-contractor on the site, said to be Kwame Nkrumah's brother, approached me with an envelope obviously holding money, a bribe to persuade me to augment his due measurement payment certificate. He made a fatal mistake, I fired him on the spot. It has always been anathema to me to have any connection with such practices, very common in the contracting business, where some contractors themselves paid very large sums of money and other inducements to obtain contracts; business but disgusting! One such contract I was involved with valued at £12 million, (not so much nowadays), was obtained by a suitcase of money and a very beautiful woman. It was not a particularly happy enterprise. My would be briber, reported me to Freddie as having demanded bribes, Freddie was very forthright and threw the man out, the latter muttering threats of putting juju on me. This could be done in many ways with effigies etc., but the most usual way was to bury a special object under a path known to be trod by the person. I felt a little disturbed and went to bed that night with the old, wartime souvenir, Luger pistol under my pillow. I was woken by a crash at my door whereupon I fired the gun. The 9mm cupro-nickel-jacketed bullet went through the door, ricocheted off a wall into the bathroom penetrating the bath, going right around my very drunk friend Hutch. Next day the pistol was very promptly disposed of.

I was asked to look after an African grey parrot, a quite expensive bird, which was to follow its owner on BOAC a few days later. Like Long John Silver he used to walk round with it perched on his shoulder, so did I and off it flew, up and up out of sight. Two days later I was standing around on the same spot, a great fluttering over my head and polly parrot landed on my shoulder; promptly popped into its travelling cage and away to catch the plane. Some years later I looked after another polly for a departing friend, who was posted from Jordan to Bahrain. I was alone at the time and polly was great company, she would sit on my shoulder repeating, 'Drink of whisky, drink of whisky,' dipping into the glass with gusto. She continued to say this, in my voice, for several months after rejoining her owners. With her crusher-like beak she caused great damage to the doors and furniture, when out of her cage.

We had a riot on the university site over pay, the men donned their native dress and armed with spears threatened us and caused some damage. A little old Hausa policeman arrived with his rifle and stool, sat in the middle of the campus and that was that. The Hausas, a warlike people, used as police and soldiers, were much feared. Some boys were clever thieves, could remove the wheels from a truck in a guarded area without being observed. The site office had two watchmen armed with bows and poisoned arrows, even so the safe was stolen one night. During my period of construction part of the area I had surveyed was allocated as the sewage disposal works and I had the pleasure to partly design and to commence the work. The resident architect was a very experienced gentleman, unfortunately our Project Manager and he were at loggerheads, not even speaking. When I was leaving the architect said, 'Whatever shall I do when you are not here?' Posted with the same company to Baghdad I

THE MIDDLE EAST

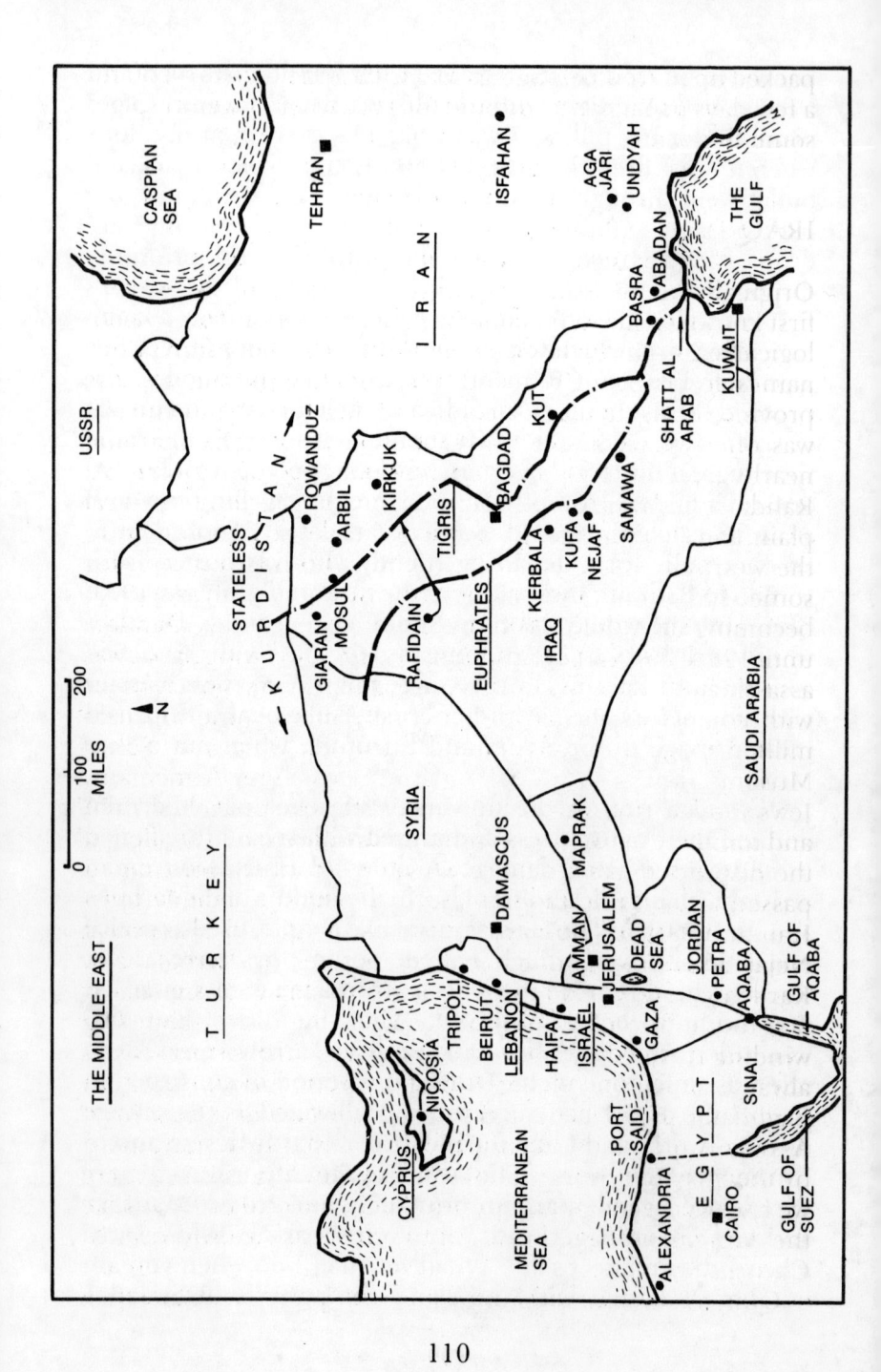

packed up my few belongings and with some regrets set off for a few days in England en route for Iraq where I was to spend some five years.

IRAQ 1952 - 1957

Originally know as Mesopotamia, the cradle of the world's first known civilization, containing many important archaeological sites, Ninevah, Babylon, Arbil, Ur and Palmyra etc, names featuring in the Old Testament. Ninevah was the province of Agatha Christie's archaeologist husband and she was often there, living in a Chinese style pagoda house at nearby Mosul. Iraq centres around the twin rivers, Al Rafidain, Euphrates and Tigris, providing a fertile central plain; mountainous to the north and east and plain desert to the west. Occupied by the Turks, the Ottoman Empire, for some 400 years, Iraq was freed by the British in 1917, becoming a Hashemite Kingdom, under a British mandate until 1932. The Kingdom ended in 1958 when King Faisal was assassinated, since when Iraq has had a socialist government with communist leanings. The population, some fourteen million people equally divided between Shia and Sunni Muslims, Kurds in the mountain areas, some Armenians, Jews and Assyrians. In the southern desert are the holy shrines and tombs of the Shia sect, prophets who were out-rivalled in the dispute over inheritance when the Prophet Mohammed passed away. Shia Muslims came as pilgrims, mainly from Iran and Pakistan, to visit the tombs of Ali and Hussein at Nejaf and Kufa and other holy shrines at Kerbala and Kardemain. Dead bodies are brought by ship to Basra and by taxi to the burial grounds at Nejaf, in bundles wrapped in winding sheets, carried on the roof racks. The Armenians as always the best jewellers special silver filigree work in Baghdad), shoemakers, tailors, etc., clever and industrious. Assyrians, not many, were probably, mistakenly, patronised by the British Administration (similarly in Yugoslavia, where we backed the wrong house, the Cetniks instead of Tito). Like the Armenians they were Christians with their own form of Christianity.

Quite a few Jews, some professionals, many in the lucrative

date trade based on Basra; I suppose most left Iraq in 1958. My dentist in Baghdad was a Jew, a good dentist too, he had been an inmate of a German concentration camp during the Second World War, a lucky survivor. One day, sitting in his waiting room, separated from the surgery by an opaque glass partition, I was aware of an awful commotion going on behind the glass, a patient having a very bad time! The dentist told me afterwards, it was the German Ambassador! It is, I suppose, rare to evince such strong feelings, but such a case also happened in Baghdad to an engineer working with me in the same company. He was a pilot in the Australian Air Force, shot down and captured by the Japanese; he spoke little of his appalling sufferings in captivity, working in coal mines in Japan; tough, he survived, but was even after several years swallowing a variety of medicinal capsules. One evening we were in a cinema when some Japanese came in, poor Tony nearly passed out; I said to him, 'Tell me the worst thing I can say in Japanese.' I shouted this out and away trooped the little men. In all fairness I must say I have met some Japanese since and found them to be very polite, intelligent and of course, clever and industrious. Similarly with Germans whom as a race I quite like; the Hitler 'bad guy', will, I am sure, one day be replaced by a certain 'no mean man', there is a very close comparison vis-a-vis 'Bogey' Bonaparte and Mr Schickelgruber! A very rich Jew I met socially was in the date export business and was developing a process for manufacturing rayon material from dates via acetates. Shalom B had the details for this operation and the equipment involved written in French, which he asked me to translate into English. We became good friends; he had a very beautiful statuesque daughter who was attending the Sorbonne, frequently travelling by air to Paris, she was always vigorously searched by Customs, even body searches. She was in fact quite scornfully amused. In 1959 I ran into Shalom B in the foyer of the Dorchester Hotel in London, he had left Iraq following the coup, leaving concealed, he told me, in his house in Baghdad, a large amount of valuables. As I was on leave, I said, 'I will go for them!' In spite of our association I am sure he could not bring himself to trust anyone in such matters. He went himself and was never heard of again.

The Kurds are a fine race of mountain people living in the

1954 IRAQ KIRKUK.
The Burning Bush – Moses eternal Gas Fires

1956 IRAQ.
Lala Ali Khan at Rowanduz, Kurdistan

mountainous regions through Turkey, Iraq and into Iran. They are Muslims and their language is a modified form of Iranian written in a mixture of Arabic or Cyrillic script. They tend to be nomadic herdsmen but have some colourful villages, particularly Rowanduz in Iraq. There is no actual Kurdish state but they have for centuries, even up to today, resisted successfully all attempts to subjugate them. Like the Afghans, Vietnamese and the Turks, the latter in 1914-18 at the Dardonelles, such people on their home ground are undefeatable. The Kurds have a lovely, very large, white species of working dog, very fierce. One hesitated to leave the security of the car when they were around. In 1941 the Germans landed a squadron of fighters and considerable transport planes at Mosul to arm the Kurds to rebel against Iraq. The situation was obviously from the military angle, logistically untenable, but the Kurds received ample supplies of ammunition and weapons, including machine-guns and automatic rifles. When I was there in 1955 frequently could be heard bursts of fire for sport. I have seen Kurds prone on their backs with the rifle, or light machine-gun held along the barrel with the knees and feet, a novel but effective aiming position. The great Kurdish leader Ali Khan was lured from Rowanduz into Iran and assassinated, some time in the 30s; his widow Lala Ali Khan carried on as leader (I have a crayon sketch of Lala and her daughter made in 1956). Kurdish women have much more freedom in society than is normal in Muslim countries.

Before I went to Mosul I was for some time constructing new roads, drainage etc., in a new Baghdad suburb and there a man called Rashid Ali was pointed out to me; he was in liaison with the Germans in 1941. German educated and trained, a small club-footed man, with a very large, tall, blonde German wife. I mentally dubbed him Seiss Inquart after the German governor of occupied Holland, also a club-foot, as was Goebbels; the Dutch called their man 'six and quarter', some slur on his name and limping gait. Another time I met up with a German Finance Minister, also club-footed; Germans seem to have been partial to such deformities. In 1927 oil was found in Kirkuk, beginning an era of prosperity, not comparable with Saudi Arabia, but enough to embark on a programme of development, infrastructure, roads, bridges, flood control, the latter most essential as the annual floods by the twin rivers devastated fertile land and rendered much unusable for ever. When I arrived such developments were in full swing with many projects in hand managed by British and German contractors. There was bitumen at Ghiarah, near Mosul, used by the Babylonians and other ancient peoples for jointing bricks and tiles, still sound to this day, known in Arabic as 'ghiah', of course essential for the road programmes. I flatter myself that I got along very well with the Iraqis, learnt their dialect and customs, which I strictly observed and respected.

In 1966 I visited an Iraqi Trade Fair in Tripoli, Libya and using my Iraqi Arabic, was made very welcome and my wife and I were showered with gifts. So KLM from Schipol, first-class in those days, until a wise company chairman said, 'I will pay for the champagne, all to travel Economy Class.' Got to know Schipol rather well as the personnel people appeared to favour KLM! Baghdad and the far from modern Semiramis Hotel, much favoured by the contractors men, terraced up to the bank of the Tigris, a very romantic setting, the air highly scented by a perfume compounded by jasmine, urine, arak and women. Baghdad a great oasis and caravanserai; coming in after a long spell in the desert was a great joy, in anticipation of the delights ahead. The company had a very well set up organization, as opposed to operating from the UK, using a local title for UK tax purposes. A head office, plant yard and stores in Baghdad, with the general manager, a Christian Scientist, seldom seen outside the city, but obviously was a capable administrator. At the time we were three site engineers, an Australian, a Welshman and self, the former two preferring to commute from Baghdad over long journeys rather than stay on site. I always preferred to live on the job. With my jeep and small belongings, I set out for Hillah-Kufa-Nejaf, which roads were to be my responsibility. At Hillah, near to Babylon, I had a contract with a local merchant, dealing in sand, concrete aggregates, road and building stone, Hadji Usta Ali Jaber, who became a very helpful friend. Usta, a coolie at the time, during the 1914-18 war, saved a British Army General from drowning when his car ran into the Euphrates; this set him up as an albeit small contractor, but quite successful and well liked. The first section of the road from Hillah up to the Euphrates at Kufa was through a fertile area with good soil for embankments, there being few cuts, no bridges but frequent reinforced concrete culverts. After Kufa towards Nejaf was pure desert, loose sand which had to be contained for the road width by imported soil shoulders. On top of the formation, which was carefully watered and rolled, a pitched limestone base some twenty centimetres thick was laid by hand, flat surfaces, about twelve centimetres across, downwards and the upper spaces filled with broken pieces down to dust. Bituminous surfacing was carried out in two layers, when the road base was finished, using a Barber Greene mixing plant and finisher, brought up from the depot in Baghdad.

The supervising authority from Hillah was the Public Works Department, quite amenable, requiring only a little generosity and entertainment in the coffee shops. From Kufa it was the Development Board, whose site representative was then a Dutch engineer. He spent most of his time in Baghdad, but when visiting the site, was unnecessarily harsh and critical, so much so that I took a very serious step and stopped the works. The reaction from the chief engineer of the Development Board was very swift, he himself having visited the site and was quite satisfied. The Dutch engineer was removed and replaced by an Australian, who took up residence in Kufa and was an altogether different kettle of fish. I rented an old Arab house, quite primitive, fed myself using a pressure cooker, lived rough, only went to Baghdad when I had an eye injury, and for eighteen months lived a monastic life saving most of my salary of necessity. One could purchase alcohol in the form of arak distilled from dates, not very pleasant, smelling and tasting of aniseed, very, very powerful. Zalowi, made from grape juice was much preferable to mastaki. Labour was good and plentiful, wages low, subsistence for the poorly paid, unleavened bread, dates and cheese, very sweet black tea and sometimes Turkish coffee. There were headmen, tindals, semi-skilled, and masons for stone or concrete. I had two supervisors, one a Sikh, a very fine fellow, fierce and warlike, much feared by the Iraqis. In 1917 a Sikh cavalry brigade advanced from Basra along the Euphrates and were ambushed, with heavy losses at Kut-al-Amara. The brigade went up the river slaughtering all they encountered; a friend of my father's was at Kut at the time. The other foreman was an Iraqi, well experienced in road works from his service with the Public Works Dept; he drank heavily and first thing each morning would consume from the shell half-a-dozen raw eggs, to sober up from the night's debauch. The Sikh, Puran Singh, one day literally saved my life when I was threatened at pistol point by two Kuwaitis I had stopped from driving over our unfinished road; he took them both by the neck from behind and simply said, 'I will kill you both.' They desisted, to my relief. We were at the time commencing work at 4 am to avoid the immense heat of the day (in summer the Iraqi desert temperature will rise to forty-five degrees Centigrade, often with dreadful sand storms), and one morning I had reason to upbraid him for something left undone. Puran, a very proud man, upped and left, such a pity!

We had very little plant, road rollers, water tankers with spray bars, materials hauled by the suppliers, otherwise pick, shovel and wheelbarrows. Donkeys with panniers distributed materials along the road, primitive but very effective, their little hooves were efficient compactors of the earth shoulders! One magnificent piece of plant was an ancient road roller, eight tons, three-wheeled, from the Aveling Barford stable. According to the elderly Kurdish driver it first saw service on a road in the Iraq mountains from Arbil to Rowandiz in 1928, constructed by a New Zealand engineer who wrote a very interesting book, *Road through Kurdistan*. The old roller had a horizontal single cylinder, diesel engine, probably twelve inches diameter bore and three feet long. The engine was started by a hot wick plug inserted into the cylinder head when lighted. The wick was the same as used in the old type French cigarette lighters, red-cotton, coarse string, probably impregnated with a solution of potassium nitrate, which burnt like a fuse. No electrics; an inertia starter, wound up by a cranked handle to a fair speed, was then engaged with the fly wheel, a massive exposed affair, hopefully starting the engine. A daily battle for the driver and his oiler mate. One morning the driver was flung up in the air by a backfire, which occurred often, and injured. He had been ruptured several times and this was his swan song. The oiler took over and did the job very well. For water we relied on the river using mechanical pumps; on the river banks were ancient Archimedes screws and chain buckets powered by donkeys or water buffaloes, a practice for centuries; the buckets were fabricated from animal hides.

The Middle East manager visited Kufa only once, accompanied by a director from London who was shocked by my living conditions; as a result I received from Baghdad an old kerosene-powered refrigerator, a well-worn carpet and some jars of home-made marmalade from the manager's wife. Late one dusky evening King Fiesal drove by when I was packing up for the day. He slowed down and called out, 'Hello, old chap, how goes it?' Harrow and Sandhurst I believe, like all the Hashemite born monarchs, as is King Hussein of Jordan. To obtain funds for pay etc., I had to draw via Usta Jakar in Hillah as there were no banks; I used to travel back to Kufa at night for security reasons, there were bandits on the road, Usta Jakar had been held up, did not stop and a rifle bullet fired through his car door tore away a large chunk of his leg, crippling him. I found one night three men with rifles blocking my way. I accelerated the jeep and rushed on; they scattered and did not shoot. In Hillah was a small YMCA run by a Muslim and his wife, where one could get a cheap night's rest and a meal, nearly always eggs and chips and the ubiquitous creme caramel pudding. The YMCA was established there for tourists visiting Babylon. I never encountered any.

Officially designated engineer, one was in fact cook and bottle washer, agent and project manager; apart from surveying, setting out, control of the works, payment of labour and suppliers, there was measurement for valuation, accounts, weekly reports, none of the staff normally to be found, albeit on larger contracts, a full life with a sense of personal achievement, the roads grew. The materials supplier in Nejaf was a very honest quarry contractor, Hadji Abid al Haddad, a good friend, never any question of cheating or malpractice. It is unfortunately always necessary to employ checkers to give receipts for loads delivered and there the opportunity occurs to falsify tickets. It is, however, with careful observation, not difficult to spot when this is occurring, a changing pattern is noticeable. Often it is necessary to relieve checkers from their not poorly paid jobs

1953 IRAQ. Kut Road

1954 IRAQ
Trade Fair
BOAC sign tower

SESIDI TEMPLE MOSUL IRAQ
1954. Sesidis worship Satan. Note serpent on wall

and in one case in Hillah I caused a man to be imprisoned, caught out in a considerable fraud. On an airfield at Mosul I had to receive and measure two stockpiles of stone, each 20,000 cubic metres, quite a responsibility.

One early evening I had a nice present, walking out of the sunset from Nejaf, a lady carrying a few belongings, I asked her where she was going – to Kufa. There were no hotels nor any other such accommodation so I took her to my shack. Lily E-S, Dutch from Amsterdam, a traveller, landscape and portrait painter, lawyer turned artist for preference; she stayed with me on many occasions in Kufa, Baghdad, Kirkuk, Mosul and Iran and I with her in Amsterdam. Lily was divorced from her husband with whom she had lived for some years in the Dutch East Indies. During the war and the German occupation of Holland, she assisted Jews to hide and to escape and was ironically betrayed by one and imprisoned in the notorious Ravensbrück concentration camp, one of the worst; she survived, the only physical effect being oedema of the legs, which one could overlook. A very good woman to whom I was most grateful for her feminine companionship, combined with talent and intelligence, I find these characteristics most attractive in the female of the species.

For a mile into Nejaf the road was a dual carriageway, with kerbs, footpaths and lighting standards, complete and ready for asphalt surfacing when I discovered a frightful error! The division between the carriageways was three metres wide and to my horror I suddenly realized that it was constructed only two metres wide at the city end, tapering over a mile, a chain man's error. Nothing, but frightfully obvious to the trained observer. For two days I was as worried as I have ever been. What to do? Too costly to rectify, so in the end I said and did nothing and I don't suppose it was ever noticed. Such penetrating worry can easily kill, as happened to a friend a few years later in London. Again out of the desert up Sheba's Highway I encountered a lone camel rider, exchanged salaams and he rode on. Hadji Abid said it was Glubb Pasha (Pasha – military commander), later commander of King Hussein of Jordan's armed forces. Whilst carrying out some work at Muasker al Rashid military airfield, outside Baghdad, I discovered that Captain Glubb was station adjutant there in 1923. Shia Muslims came as pilgrims from all over for the religious festivals of Id al Fitr and Id al Adha, converging on Nejaf. The processions were fabulous, flagellation being the main theme, pilgrims in the lesser act flogging their naked bodies with chains and in the greater torment, striking their foreheads with the edge of a khanjar, a dagger-type knife, drawing blood and frequently falling down unconscious or dead. Mothers would hold their babies under the dripping blood. At night a very colourful scene was that of a man with a huge palm tree trunk carried across his shoulders, burning at both ends, twirling like a Dervish.

So my contract completed, I returned to Baghdad, to return to Kufa at the end of the maintenance period, the only repair work required was a small section of the asphalt surfacing which had failed due to overheating of the stone aggregate. Hadji Abid gave me his photograph and a great 'brass' finger ring embossed with the Royal Crown of Iraq and a letter. From the Tomb of Ali the Seyid wrote me a letter of thanks for lending a water tanker for the pilgrims' use and literally for keeping my nose clean in their holy places. Showing the ring to my father he said, 'That is not brass, it's gold!' It was very heavy. These mementoes were lost during the Turkish invasion of Cyprus in 1974. At Baghdad I carried out some extensions to the Alwiyah Club, then a very exclusive one, mainly European, where in addition I obtained a room, living in unaccustomed luxury. A period followed on a road near the Iranian border, Bacuba-Jallowlah, to finish off a nearly completed project. Bacuba was a centre for oranges and in Iraq were known as 'bacuba', as opposed to 'portugal' elsewhere. Of course, citrus fruits originated in China. Whilst on this job a labourer roped one of the watchmen to the railway line, when the body was discovered cut into three pieces by the night train from Baghdad. This was seemingly a family feud, the labourer fled but was caught and shot by the watchman's relatives. With an estimator from London I carried out a survey for a road 120 miles through the mountains, Jallowlah to Derbendikhan, beautiful, rugged country, my companion was enthralled, never having been abroad before. Another company, Balfour Beatty, was awarded the work and in fact offered me the position of project manager, which I turned down. The road included a one mile long tunnel under an otherwise impassable mountain range. Back in Baghdad there were a number of relatively small jobs to work on; new suburbs roads and drainage; Iraq Spinning and Weaving factory extension and concrete internal roads; aprons and hangars at Muasker Al Rashid military airfield, works and resurfacing at Baghdad civil airport etc. A busy, interesting time.

I was sent off to Mafrak in Jordan to assess the desirability of involvement in the construction of an airfield. Mafrak was a desert strip, without facilities, used by the RAF and BOAC for refuelling. From RAF Habbanyah, in Iraq, I got a lift to Amman where the wing commander provided transport to the site. There was little to see but the dirt strip and a fuel store, but sticking out like a sore thumb, there was no water for many miles, all water for the works must be trucked in, from a river source I judged to be inadequate. In order to achieve the necessary soil and base compaction, sufficient water is essential. My report was considered sufficient to turn the job down. Some years later I met a director of the local firm who took the job. My predictions were correct and money was lost. However a miracle occurred which enabled them to finish the job, without incurring further losses. In a dry desert area it suddenly rained very heavily for several days! A seat in a taxi took me to Jerusalem on my way home, I suppose that there was at that time no flight from Amman to Baghdad. Arrived in Jerusalem, then a divided city, but with the holy Christian places on the Arab side, I could not find any accommodation, all hotels absolutely full. Accosted by a young Arab he said, 'Come with me to my father's hotel,' which turned out to be the Arab Hotel, minus all five stars, at the St Stephen's Gate. The owner was delighted to see an Englishman after so many years. Asking why the hotels were full he said, 'But didn't you know? Today is Good Friday!' I had to stay until Easter Sunday and the boy took me over the Easter routine of Bethlehem, Nazareth, and the stations of the cross. So in fact I became a *hadji* of Jerusalem, a title which was in fact used by some pilgrims. At the airport, the emigration officer said, 'Sir, your passport has expired.' A kindly official he let me proceed, saying I could renew my passport in Beirut. Beirut, Easter Monday, the British Embassy firmly closed, no chance, so I decided to risk getting into Iraq and caught a plane, my passport undetected.

Back to the odd jobs which gave much pleasure, I often look back on those days with nostalgia, I was my own boss so far as the work was concerned, no other expatriates to handle, it was always much better on one's own with local staff and labour. Expatriates were very often troublesome. With the Australian engineer, we went to live in a small pension run by a French lady, Lucille. One night she came to my room, unforgettably wearing gold-trimmed, black satin pyjamas which slid off and so to bed. This was the greatest and most shattering love of my life and of hers, devastating, a union of souls and bodies, an *orage,* without exaggeration.

Late spring, the snows melting in the mountains, the Tigris, swollen, brown, surging water, perilously near the tops of the protective bunds which were jelly like underfoot, Baghdad was surrounded by a system of earth bunds, floods were already spreading in the outlying areas particularly southwards towards the road to Kut, constructed on high embankments, which were being threatened by the ever increasing depth of surrounding water. With a few men I was busy pegging rush mats along the slopes to save the road. We were cut off from behind where the road was breached. Providentially, a friend, manager of Balfour Beatty, who had boats, came out and rescued us, no possibility to get back swimming, the waters dangerously swirling round in powerful surges. A vital bund was breached a few miles from Baghdad, seriously threatening the city's million inhabitants, it being already surrounded by the flood. My company was asked to help and I assembled some three thousand casual coolies and great quantities of sandbags. Working continuously night and day for ten days, gradually narrowing the gap from both sides until, the speed of the flow increased by the venturi effect, after a tremendous fight, the hole was closed, a big Dutch boy's elbow in the dyke. The biggest problem was to pay the army of labourers after each eight hour shift. The Iraqi Army gave us some controlling support with supplies, radio and transport communications and the prime minister visited. The whole operation cost the company £60,000, the Government said thank you very much! We were asked to look at another breach some twenty-five miles upstream. Having decided it needed sheet piling, I approached Siemens who were building a bridge over the

Tigris and had the necessary piling equipment. They refused to have anything to do with it. Flood control projects continued for many years and I believe the centuries' old problem is now overcome. One of the most impressive schemes was at Wadi Thartar, a huge overflow basin excavated by Balfour Beatty, during my time. Just after the flood panic came a cable from London simply saying 'Proceed to Karachi immediately.' Just that after two years in Iraq. Few belongings packed, goodbye to madame and away. At Karachi airport saw my first sight of the gigantic shed, built to house the ill-fated airship R-101, which crashed in France, 5 October 1931 (anniversary of my birthday), stupendous. At immigration, my medical certificate for cholera was filled in but unsigned; no way could I be allowed in! After some hours when another plane arrived I scribbled a signature in the book and mingled with the passengers. This time, fortunately, unremembered and with hardly a glance, I was through. A taxi to 'the best hotel' in Karachi, which I believe was the Metropole. At the reception desk I asked if I had a booking, no! Cursing audibly the vagueness of the posting, a man by my side said, 'I believe you are looking for me, Peter Elliot.' We got to know each other very well in the following years.

The job was a reconnaissance survey of the Sui gas pipeline project from Karachi, Hyderabad, Sukkur, and hence into Baluchistan to Sui, the source, near Jacobabad. I had the section up to Sukkur and the next morning left with a hired car, driver, cook, provisions, a case of whisky and bottles of soda water, very efficiently laid on by Peter. The exercise was to follow the pipe-line route, detailing going, obstacles, access, availability of all necessaries, labour, plant and transport, materials of all kinds, etc., local customs and anything relevant to estimating the value of the work, in order to submit a tender. I decided to operate from Hyderabad some 100 miles along the route and thence cover the area to Sukkur a further 300 miles. The driver and cook, old Indian Army soldiers, took me to a rest house, a truly magnificent dwelling in beautiful grounds, all polished mahogany, brass and silver, where I was the only guest. That evening I had a visitor who introduced himself as the general manager of the Burmah Oil Company. I told him I was an engineer carrying out a survey for George Wimpey, he said, 'Good lord, what are you doing here? This is the senior judges circuit rest house.' We laughed and I stayed on. Moving on to Sukkur some days later I found also excellent accommodation thanks to my 'old soldiers'. On one occasion in Sukkur I called at the railway junction HQ to enquire regarding the availability of flat bed wagons for pipes. I was shown into a large room where there was a meeting proceeding; it turned out to be a court of enquiry into a very serious railway disaster, involving some 100 deaths. Such was the 'respect' for the British, if you can so call it, from the days of the Raj, the president interrupted the proceedings to answer my comparatively mundane questions. Respect is not the correct term, but whatever it denotes a consanguinity, a relationship even of the blood, since many of the peoples of the sub-continent are Aryan types. Whatever, one finds this in India and Pakistan and particularly when involved with them together in mutually foreign lands. The survey took about two months and apparently was successful, or at least all were pleased, including Peter. The project, however, was carried out by others. One feature on the route was the Barani Gorge, a deep, dry river bed, some two to three miles across, which became a raging torrent in the monsoon season.

Back to Baghdad to everyone's surprise, having thought to have waved me goodbye for ever. The Middle East Manager was going on leave and I was to stand in for him, besides carrying on with my current work, not too difficult since at that time we had no work going on outside the city. There was a short survey for a road from Basra to Kuwait, via a very interesting small mountain feature, Jebel Sirnam; at the time nothing matured for this proposal. In the Baghdad office we had an accountant, English, whose mother was secretary to the chairman at that time; a pleasant young man but perhaps a bit of a playboy. I came into the office one evening and found the safe wide open and telephoned around until I found him, when he came absolutely scared out of his wits. We had to check the contents and there was a very large sum of money, if I remember correctly some £90,000, being a fund from the sale of empty, steel, bitumen drums. Later there was an inquiry by our company ex fraud squad police officer, when he accused me of knowing about the fund, which I persuaded him was totally untrue. He later investigated a contract I was managing and gave me a clean report, except that a few pounds were missing from the petty cash. The office boy had gone to the bazaar to buy some small thing, the auditor said, but in that case why not a chit in the cash box recording the fact! The auditor was always welcome, fiddles were not uncommon in the construction business and it was always pleasing to get a clean report. One particular annual auditor on a large project was my neighbour in Cyprus, until he died recently; all items on site were checked, plant, materials, stores, discarded bits and pieces, cash and site account ledgers. On one occasion he could not locate all of twelve concrete vibrators, small, mobile items of plant, so I said we would have to go round to check in the evening, when work was over, which he did.

I was considered at the time to take charge of the installation of an oil drilling rig in the Gulf, one of the early ones, with three legs, always an unstable object. The job was given to another and the platform did overturn, so perhaps old providence was taking a hand once more.

At breakfast one morning I felt an irritation in the back of my right hand and pulled out a cactus thorn about an inch long which must have been there since the Gold Coast, without any previous indication of a foreign body. It then festered and swelled up alarmingly to the size of a golf ball. A French doctor staying with Madame, lanced it and put on a plaster bandage, which remained until I went on leave. We obtained the contract for the Baghdad British Trade Fair ground preparation, roads and pavings, temporary buildings, exhibition stands, etc., for myself all very new departures in the business. The British director of International Trade Fairs was very much a professional, knew exactly what was required. One personal headache was a sign for BOAC, some sixty feet high on four two inch scaffold tubes, ledged and braced, it was OK in the event. A British TV firm, Pye I believe, had a fairly permanent studio erected and I found for them, in a direct line, a transmitter position on the Ziggurat some sixty miles north of Baghdad. A Ziggurat is a tall tapering structure with a winding outside stairway, probably Assyrian, similar in significance to the Egyptian pyramids. It was disastrous for Pye, if it was them, as their TV sets did not arrive in time and Philips, whose did, scooped the market.

Due for home leave, feeling somewhat jaded, (Lucille was very jealous and made sure that I had no desires left over for others), off I went to my parents' home in Surrey. The company doctor, a very fashionable Welbeck Street Irishman, profoundly experienced, Rolls-Royced, looked at my hand and packed me off to the Blue Sisters' Hospital in Lambeth Road. The area was stripped down to the bone and skin grafted, some two weeks' incarceration and then out to enjoy my leave, including a quick visit to Kufa Lily in Amsterdam. I cultivated the girl next door, nothing serious, just good fun, we still correspond. Back to work and a new project, the first section of the Baghdad-Kut road, some thirty miles long, over a flat plain, generally infertile, due to flooding. The route passed close to an ancient building at Cetisphon, a mathematically perfect parabola in shape, some thirty metres high at the peak and 100 metres long closed at one end; monument to a long-departed Persian monarch. In a remarkably good state of preservation, straw-bonded, sun-baked clay bricks. A blind beggar sat always at the open end, playing on a primitive flute, the resonance was incredibly pure. The road followed the old alignment and the problem was to maintain the flow of traffic, quite considerable, being the only main road to the south and no possibility of diversions, except essentially at bridges and culverts, due to the nature of the surrounding terrain. Starting at the beginning, the city end, with an office and yard some five miles away, earthworks and the reinforced concrete small bridges going ahead. The concrete work I put in charge of a young engineer fresh from England, keen and capable; he arrived wearing a magnetic compass on a wrist strap! The supervising engineer for the Development Board came on site at the beginning and without any preliminaries, demanded a house to be built and furnished to his requirements and a car of his choice. I was utterly disgusted and said, 'All right, but I must consult my director,' who ruled that we were forced to comply, but only provided the cost was met by false payment certificates. The engineer ended up in an Iraqi prison. On the personal front Lucille decided that we were destroying each other and I must go. An absolutely shattering blow, indescribable. However grim, one had to accept fate and I moved out. As work progressed the culverts were used by travellers and their wives, whom presumably they prostituted. For currency they carried carpets slung over the shoulder. I bought a small Isfahan rug for £50, which I still have, said to be quite valuable, fortunately not taken in 1974 by the soldiery. Kufa Lily came on her way to Tibet, to seek an interview with the Buddhist Dalai Lama, who was then, before the Chinese came, living in Lhasa. She was very impressed by the great spiritual presence of the current living Buddha and also sought our joint astrological predictions, from a German monk, interesting, but like such things could apply to anyone.

Due to inter-departmental rivalry the Middle East office was taken over by another section of the company, desirous of having a go overseas. As a result of this, I was replaced by one of their men and for a short while did some small jobs around and about. One day I ran into the then Minister for Defence, a general whom I had met over Muasker al Rashid military airfield. He said he wanted Mosul and Kirkuk airfields to be reconstructed, lengthened, new taxiways and hardstandings and drainage, details of which we there and then agreed, literally on the back of a postcard. A simple priced bill of quantities, comprising also the specifications was rapidly agreed and in a few days the whole operation was implemented and I caught the Orient Express, which started at Baghdad, for Mosul. As good or bad luck would have it, as the train pulled out I saw Lucille on the platform. The famous train was very exciting, the journey being overnight, very slow due to the poor condition of the permanent way, arriving at Mosul for breakfast. Very well appointed single sleeping cabins with toilet, the guard offering half bottles of brandy at a fairish price, mine turned out to be Hennessy with the seal broken and a verminous brew inside! At Mosul I at once found a house right at the end of the existing runway belonging to an air force pilot; I was to be resident in Mosul with a watching brief over Kirkuk. Two Kurdish brothers appeared, stone contractors capable of supplying the huge quantity of stone required and price being competitive, they went to work. The next day they appeared with a cardboard box containing a brand new .45 Webley revolver, as big as a cannon, saying, 'A man in your position must have a gun.' I refused the kind offer but they, thinking it was not good

1956 IRAQ MOSUL
A mosque built on the top of King Sennacherib's Tomb, said to protect the King's wealth in gold and jewels. Mosul airport is situated on the plain, *bottom right*.

enough, brought a very smart Bereta 7.62 automatic, which I kept. The convoy from Baghdad arrived and away we went to a very smooth start. There was a general foreman, Irish, typical civil engineering man and a newly-married engineer. Both lasted a matter of weeks; as I pointed out before, expatriates are often troublesome. The newly-wed just could not bear being separated from his bride; the foreman brought his girlfriend, she wanted to get back to the smoke, so!

Mosul was delightful, green and fertile towards the mountains, storks nesting on all the chimney tops in the spring; rushing mountain torrents, colourful Kurds. Visits to

Kirkuk every week where there was a not very active agent with a very nubile blonde wife. Accommodation was difficult, the railway rest house the best, far from good, or a very sleazy hotel with ghastly food. The Iraqi Air Force had some Sea Furies at Mosul, a naval version of the Spitfire with a radial engine, dodgy to land, as the torque turned them hard to port and dangerously so, off the runway. The CO was a Lt. Col. and the pilots Captains or Lieuts., good chaps, one a close relative of King Feisel. In 1958 during the revolution, I learnt that most of them were executed by hanging. They were mad about foreign women and were somewhat successful with the oil company wives. Receiving news that my father was very ill, I went home for two weeks to say goodbye. He died soon after I returned to Mosul. Under the new regime I was not entitled to the air fare, nor my salary, during my absence, a little harsh considering the hardships endured in the interests of the company. The new director obviously thought so as well and reimbursed me out of his own pocket.

One feature in Iraq I have not encountered elsewhere, is the sirdab, a cellar under the house going down two or three storeys, usually until water is arrived at, cool and quiet in summer. Lily used to visit with a couple of young wives in their sirdab for coffee mornings, she told me that they very proudly displayed to her, beautiful, tattooed butterflies on their backsides, much admired by the husband. To divert, at the dentist's today (I have spent many visits and much money on dentistry and consequently still have my own teeth, very much worthwhile), he said his son was learning to parachute and had achieved a very dangerous jump from 400 feet. I told him of a friend an army dentist, who was trained to parachute to treat Wingate's Chindits in Burma. His story concerned a Gurkha regiment whose colonel announced that they were to jump out of airplanes, 'But Sahib, we shall be killed!'

The colonel said, 'But not with parachutes!'

'Oh, OK if we are going to have those things.'

My dentist countered with the story of a Greek soldier from Soli, men noted for bravery; at a barbers' for a shave, the barber said, 'Such a brave man does not need soap,' and proceeded to shave him dry!

As work progressed Iraqi Airways started a daily service using Dove aircraft and one day as RAF jet Meteor trainer landed. The squadron leader pilot complimented us on the runway and offered me a ride, the radio crackled and he said, 'Too bad, I have to go back to Habbaniyah immediately, but I will show you how the plane can climb.' He did and went up almost vertically. So Mosul and Kirkuk finished successfully and work had dried up in the area, as often happened after several years of contracts, farewell Iraq.

A SPELL IN THE UK

During my leave from Iraq, Peter Elliot, of the Sui gas pipeline survey, contacted me and when we met he offered me a job in the UK. This suited me fine, as my mother was terminally ill. Peter was then a director for the contractors whose logo is the four men on a rope. He wanted me to set up a planning department and improve quality control, particularly in the field of concrete, on a number of major office block contracts in the London area. Set up at first in the prestigious head office in Park Lane, I subsequently moved to an oil company's building under construction in the Barbican, work for which had commenced and was troublesome. My job to help things along and to maintain, at the same time, the other functions of planning in the group. The building was bounded exactly by four City streets, where building lines must be absolutely maintained. Larsen sheet piled and excavated down to the lovely London blue clay, to a depth where the Walbrook River was exposed. When the foundations were ready for the structural steel framing a serious setting out error was discovered. The consequences of not being able to correct this situation without it being known would have been disastrous and very costly. Working in a portable hut with rock drills, over the whole of a five day Easter holiday day and night, all was corrected. I had to ensure myself that there was no structural risk involved. It was at this time a great opportunity to use new methods of construction: tower cranes, concrete pumps, packaged bricks and many other developments. One significant factor was the effect of the increase in heights of buildings from the hitherto statutory limit of 120 feet, vertigo occurred when going over the accustomed height. I became involved mainly in work below ground; I designed and executed several deep basement temporary supporting works, very interesting and the experience came in very useful in later years. I had designed one such supporting work for a large office block, adjacent to the Old Bailey, very critical, any collapse being out of the question. At the time I escorted Peter on a visit to Germany, Hanover and Leipzig Fairs and to look at new construction in Berlin, in spring of 1958.

We picked up information on quite a few good new types of plant and machinery and placed some orders. Accommodation was desperately short in Hanover and we were booked into a small hotel, the bedroom had one large double bed! In the morning I awoke and there in front of my eyes was a pinkly shining bald head! When we returned I was sent to Sunderland to erect a small factory extension for the family business of one of the company's directors, the manufacturer of copper and bronze pipings and fittings for ships. Doxfords Engines works were opposite and their chief engineer, blue-serge suited and bowler-hatted, showed me around the works and also over a ship under construction. The congested working conditions in the engine room were unbelievable, the fitters must be contortionists, cramped into spaces appearing to be inaccessible. In the works the engineer told me that I would see processes not to be found anywhere else in the world; one of these was profile cutting of twelve inch thick steel plate to produce giant connecting rods. As I recall the Doxford Marine Engine is a twin cylinder, opposed, diesel-fuelled power plant, probably slow revving, ponderous but utterly reliable. Sunderland very enjoyable, nice people. Soon after I returned to London the building site opposite the Old Bailey had a road collapse, fracturing gas, water and electricity supplies. This was made more serious by the programmed visit to the area that day of Princess Margaret, accompanied by Prince Philip, the Queen at that time was in childbirth. This visit had to be cancelled and some of the adjacent buildings to be evacuated. Poor Peter Elliot died the next day, presumably from a heart attack, caused by the worry over the affair, a young, brilliant company director. It recalled my own condition over a much less serious mistake on the Kufa-Nejaf road. A court of enquiry was held by the City Dangerous Structures' Engineer, where my detailed scheme for shoring up the excavated perimeter with twelve inch die squares and trench sheets, some six diagrams indicating the procedure to be observed, were produced. The Engineer said, 'Fine, but why was it not done?' Stony silence. Perhaps it would have been if I had not been sent to Sunderland.

This period in London may seem to be unexciting, it was not, but I did feel a fish out of water, little in common with those around me. At a Technical German evening class course I met a very jolly, plump Austrian girl, married, a niece of the famous violinist, Kreisler. Two incidents come to mind, meeting her at six o'clock one evening outside Swan and Edgar's in Piccadilly, in common with many others so bent, she rushed up, slapped my face and shouted, 'What about my baby, you swine!' Another time she insisted on going to a pub frequented only by homosexuals, who were not at all amused. The husband looked me up one day, he did not object but said I was making his wife very miserable. I suppose what she wanted was unattainable. Soon after the tragic Old Bailey affair I was asked to go to India for a few months, to which I agreed, particularly as with Peter gone I had lost interest in the job. With a senior accountant for the business side, off we went to Calcutta, first of all to meet the client, the Burmah Oil Company.

INDIA 1959

We were joined in Calcutta by two representatives of our American partners who were intending to survey the route by helicopter. One of them, an ex-fighter pilot, confided in me that he hated flying as he always ran into trouble, such as forced landings and once a propeller flew off. The next day he was killed; the engine of the helicopter failed. I understand there is no way of gliding a helicopter unless the drive can be immediately disengaged. Calcutta was thrilling. The Great Eastern Hotel, where we stayed, Firpo's Restaurant and Shepherds, the Tea Planter's Hotel were very exciting. At lunch in Firpo's we saw Han Suyin, the Chinese authoress of *Love is a Many Splendoured Thing,* at a table with a truly magnificent Indian Prince, black as coal, but how handsome. At a cabaret there was an artiste calling herself Sabrina, of bosom fame, I said to her, 'But you cannot be Sabrina, you

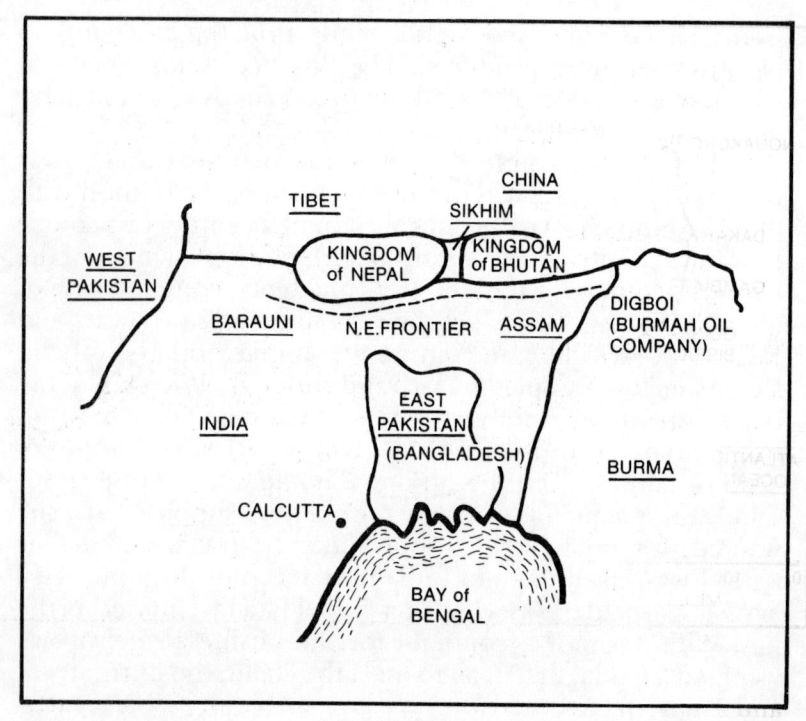

Oil pipe line

have nothing up top!'

The survey was a pleasure; Assam out of this world; the Kasaranga wild animal reserve, notices on the road, beware of cobras, keep your car windows closed; the tea plantations, most expert gardening, to be seen also in the towns, clubs and dwellings. Due to the proximity of the Chinese and doubts of their intentions, the project was abandoned by the American and British consortium. A Yugoslav contractor did complete the pipeline, payment being made to them in jute, a plant fibre used for hessian, sacking, mats etc. produced widely in India

GHANA 1959-60

Soon after returning from the trip to India, my mother died

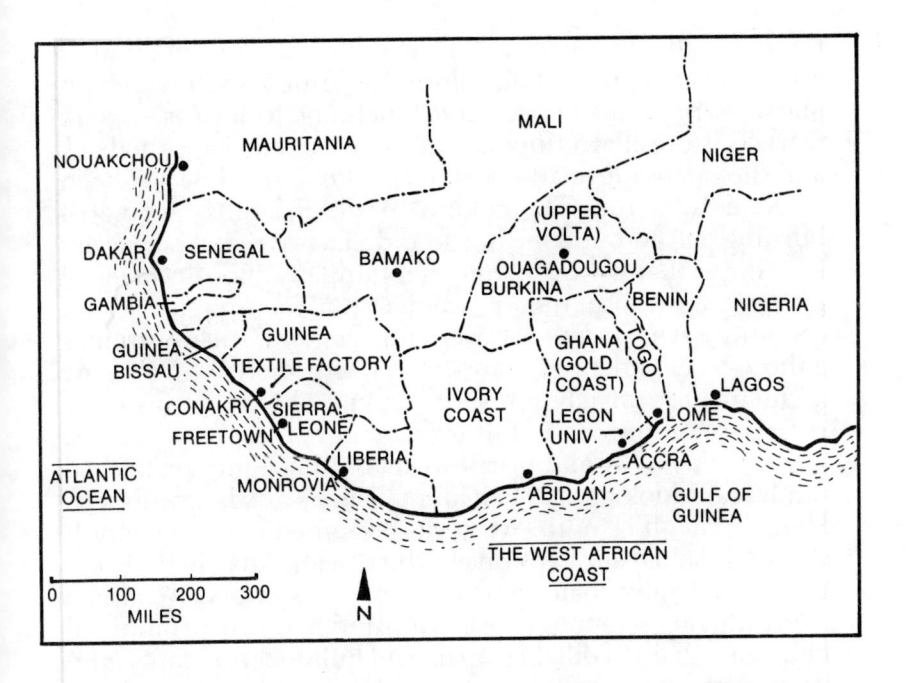

and I was free to return to my love of life in foreign parts. Offered a job in Ghana to manage a section of the West Coast International Highway from across the Volta River at Sogankope to Denu on the Togoland border, traversing what was one time German West Africa. Kwame Nkrumah was then President, after being released from jail, on independence from British rule (cf Archbishop Makarios of Cyprus, captive in the Seychelles). As in Iraq, the company had a permanent set-up in Accra, with a managing director and two other directors. It was refreshing to get back to the spicy smell of the coast and the (in the case of Ghana) cheerful black man. A less black coloured, will refer to another as, you, that black man ever there! We established ourselves in an old Public Works' Department camp at Akatsi, a village on the route, there were no towns except Lomé over the border in Togo. For staff I had a very good bunch of expatriates, put together from other works in the area, general foreman, engineer, soils engineer (most important as the road base was compacted of specially selected, red laterite soil, difficult to find in quantity), concrete foreman, accountant and quantity surveyor, visiting plant foreman, all experienced. The engineer came from another job in Sierra Leone and was allowed to bring his wife with him. She was a nice little thing, a little lonely and forlorn as we were working from dawn until after dusk. One night I came back and she ran to me nearly in hysterics, her bungalow had been invaded by a rope-like column of soldier ants. A ring of burning petrol round the house and that was that. I had a very fine diesel Land Rover, but the company had decided all others would use motor scooters or motorcycles as an economy. A mistake, not everyone can ride such machines although experienced car drivers, so there were many accidents, fortunately not very serious. The route was quite reasonable going except for several miles of black soil swamp, primaeval, smelly and occasionally the machines unearthed unpleasant looking fish like animals with bristling whiskers, living in the thick mud. We never bottomed in the section. It was suggested using explosives, a bit of a joke that; in the event the road literally floated and was quite satisfactory. We lost an earth-moving scraper in the swamp and it took the combined effort of a chain of other scrapers and bulldozers to pull it out. A quarry was opened up, necessitating explosives from Accra and a quarry master. To obtain such sources of materials such as stone and sand one had to negotiate with the chief either in his village or on the site. The chief would appear in his robes with ceremonial stool and umbrella, attended by his retinue and bargaining would commence after I presented bottles of Genever, Square Face gin, the most favoured drink. A libation poured on the ground and a few drinks and the price agreed, never very much, say £60 for a gravel pit enough for our concrete needs. On one such occasion the chief's daughter, a fine upstanding six foot maiden, wanted a ride in the Land Rover, having never been in a car before. As soon as we got going she jumped out and ran off scared witless. However one evening she came to my bungalow with a letter in pidgin English. It was Christmas Eve. The epistle said, 'Darling, I am your Christmas present, I shall need a bed, blanket, table and chair and a sewing machine,' to purchase for which I was to give her £50, I never did but she came occasionally, barefooted in the night. Snakes of course were the usual nuisance but only one expatriate was bitten, his fault, he liked playing with them; fortunately a non-poisonous grass snake. Food was not available for Europeans locally, the Africans ate cassava, a pure starch root crop, maize, ground nuts and such like. We relied on stores in bulk from Accra, frozen items in a 'chop' box with blocks of ice. To cross the wide Volta River there was a ferry which frequently broke down, when the cold supplies were delayed and ruined. The accountant was keen to get to Accra most often, so it was convenient that he looked after the commissary.

One day I went to Lomé to see a dentist for a check up and ended up the visit by giving up smoking tobacco. As a child I had with others occasionally smoked Woodbines at two old pennies for five cigarettes. The first time of course we were sick, unremarked as small boys often were. I did not seriously take up smoking until my mother said, 'I like to see a man smoking a pipe,' so I did. My father died from lung cancer, almost certainly caused by smoking, he used to roll his own cigarettes using a very strong, black tobacco.

When I went to the dentist in Lomé, an American negro, rejoicing in the name of Robert E Lee, was operating three chairs single-handed, he held a small mirror to my mouth and indicated a white line inside my lower lip. 'You are doing something you should not,' he told me, 'and only you know what.' I did know and when I left the surgery I threw away my pipe, pouch and matches. Some years later I met an American lady doctor who wrote a book entitled, *The Grass is Greener*, suggesting that some drugs, hashish and so on, were less harmful than smoking or alcohol. I never experimented with drugs nor ever met any users. However, I was cured of the habit of smoking and never felt the urge to start again and other people's smoke does not bother me.

Apart from one memorable weekend in Lomé, I had not been away from the site for nearly a year. It has always been my practice to be on the job for all working hours, all working days and that is frequently seven, no harm when there is nothing else to do. The managing director made his one and only visit, said almost nothing, the job was going very well. He reminded me of the CO of the 1st Tanks. Another director with him took me on one side and whispered, 'He is jealous, thinks you are after his job, watch out!' How right he was, a few days later I received a plane ticket. He had a reputation for dishing them out, no explanation. Rude justice, he himself had a plane ticket soon afterwards.

On the other hand, old man providence was at work again. For a short while I had been feeling unwell and on arrival at Heathrow, I literally weaved my way to a door marked with a red cross; the nursing sister inside saw me looking towards the bed and said, 'If you lie down you won't get up. Where are you going?

'To Amsterdam,' I replied.

So she told me, 'Try to make it.'

Somehow I made the Vondelstraat and Lily. She called a friend, the Director of the School of Tropical Medicine, who, after an examination said, 'Ah, something very interesting for my students; a severe case of malaria coupled with dengue fever', the malaria to recur for many years afterwards. When recovered I was told to report to London office which I did (they refused to pay the air fare from Amsterdam, which I thought was rather mean), the department were not too pleased but immediately offered me a job. An airfield under construction in Iran was in the doldrums, go and sort it out. With the responsible director I went to Tehran to meet the head of Shell, who were officially the client and having done so travelled by train to Ahwaz as I could not get a seat on a plane to Abadan. The train journey, very slow over a narrow gauge railway built by Germany, largely through hilly country, four-bunk compartments, a restaurant car with the inevitable obijo beer, which is very oily and stabilised with glycerine. Twenty-four hours to Ahwaz and taxi to the site near Agha Jari, at Umideyah, some 100 miles from Abadan.

IRAN (Before 1935, Persia)

Iran, a country of vast deserts and marshes bordered by mountain ranges to the north, east and west, and the sea to the south, variously known as the Persian Gulf, or Iranian, or Arabian Gulf. The population currently stands at some fifty million, mainly Persians, who are Aryan people, not Semites, with groups of Turks, Kurds, Armenians and Arabs, the principal nomadic tribe are the Baktiari, a colourful people who annually migrate from north to south following the grazing. Nomads are disliked by established, settled nations and in the fifties, the Shah took stringent steps to halt the migration and to force the tribes to settle. This is very well told in *The Last Migration*. The Shah literally established a line of soldiery across the country to force a halt to the Baktiari movements.

The economy prior to 1908, when oil was first discovered, was mainly agricultural, hampered by lack of rainfall. Sheep and goats abound. Iran is famous for textiles, carpets, art and handicrafts. Other industries flourished following the enormous increase in oil revenues in the seventies, particularly steel production. Iran was, with Iraq, the earliest known centre of civilization, dominated in turn by Turks and Mongols, Arabs (brought Islam,) encroached on over the centuries by Uzbeks, Afghans, British and Russians. The Kajar dynasty established the Shah rule in the eighteenth century and continued until 1980 when Ayatollah Khomeini took over. The regime was extremely repressive. Savak, the secret police, were notorious for imprisonment, torture and execution.

Some day I intend to make a study of the Iran-Iraq Gulf war of which little is known by the West, except of the naval operations to keep open the oil tanker routes, against resolute attacks against shipping involving that nasty piece of work, the Exocet missile. The airfield at Umidiyah was located on the ground by Douglas Bader, the legless RAF fighter pilot, who was then employed by Shell as a consultant. One drawback which was to prove costly, there was a 165,000 volt cable line crossing the approach path, expensive to install such cables underground. Shell were responsible for the project, but since they at that time only had need for light aircraft, such as the Dove or Fokker Friendship, and the runway was of such length and construction that it was suitable for the heaviest bombers, the B52 for example, we thought that NATO was the real client. Lack of activity on the site when I arrived was very apparent, quite a large staff, who were not energetic, nor seemingly interested, with the exception of two youngish engineers, a Scot and an Australian, first class chaps. There was also, fortunately, a competent and willing plant and transport manager, who ran an efficient workshop. The runway construction was one metre thick, random rock rubble, topped off by twenty-five centimetres of crushed stone, levelled and graded. Surfacing was a bitumen tack coat, followed by a substantial wearing course about six millimetres thick, surface dressing with fine chips rolled with smooth rollers. Very cheap and effective provided the stone base surface is smooth and even as possible. Control of the spraying is by a fifth wheel, gauging the speed and consequent volume of material delivered over the surface. The stone quarry was a shambles, the quarry foreman had in one big bang blown the mountain to pieces, instead of expertly working to face and ledge, step at a time. The net result was hand collection of the pieces in head pans, and expensive pop blasting of the larger rocks, which would not have resulted if the charges had been correctly spaced with the proper amount of explosive. Fortunately the labour force was Arab, a group from the marsh area, contiguous to the Shatt al Arab, on the opposite side to Iraq, consequently I learnt no Pharsi but my Arabic came in very useful. The company were obliged to employ a number of Iranians, particularly labourers, unsuited to the work. These were provided with large marquees and facilities for chai, and there they took their ease and collected their pay, a satisfactory arrangement all round. Two of them, however, volunteered for one of the hardest and most trying jobs, the driving of the vibrating roller which compacted the random rock base. The roller was a magnificent machine, one of the early ones, made by Stoddart and Pitt, really handled the job as nothing else seemingly could. The snag was that it tended to shake itself to bits, so I instituted half and hour's work and then maintenance which took a similar time. The two stalwarts kept it going, much credit to them. Things were going very well, the relationship with Shell improved and their representative, a Dutch engineer from being anti, became cooperative.

Suddenly a Gold Coast cactus thorn came out through my groin; difficult to understand how a piece the size of a pin can be encased in the flesh and not be apparent. I had to go into hospital at Agha Jari as my groin was immediately infected and swelled up. My three willing staff visited every night for the two weeks I was in bed, and the job kept going along. The surgeon who was to perform the operation was an army major, anxiously I asked where he qualified, Tabriz he informed me! There was it seemed a well-established medical school at Tabriz. After the operation I was submitted to periods of infra-red ray treatment (it could have been ultra-violet?), a nurse left me too long under the lamp and my abdomen was badly burnt, it never healed until I got back to Europe.

However, as far as the work was concerned the bit was between the teeth of my small gang and all went well, although somewhat painfully for me. The buildings were no problem, the usual reception areas, offices, stores, toilets, etc., fire station and refuelling point. The earthing of the fuel station was a problem, we could not at first find suitable locations for the copper rods, giving adequate earthing. These rods were connected by lines to the aircraft, to deal with static electricity, when fuelling. I had no office and operated entirely from my car, which happened to be a very likeable Ford Zodiac with an overdrive, supposedly the equivalent to the modern fifth gear. We were allowed to draw on the oil company stores at Masjed Suleyman, known as MIS, but also maintained our own stores on site. The expatriate storekeeper was an affable chap, minor public school, clergyman father, more than overfond of the bottle; as such he was a pest and was never around when stores were required. He had ingratiated himself with some of the local bigwigs and used their club. Exasperated one day by his absence, I requested the project manager to dismiss him and this was agreed. The next day a young Iranian officer came for me in a jeep and drove me off, miles into the hills. We arrived at a grim barbed wire and corrugated iron compound and I was conducted into a splendidly appointed room, sitting behind a massive desk was a young colonel, beautifully turned out, polished riding boots resting on the desk. He introduced himself as the Shah's Representative and Governor of the Province. Iran was divided into seven such provinces and this was presumably Khudistan. The colonel said, 'I am pleased that your job is progressing very well, I have a request for you not to discharge a certain employee, if you do so, then I will order the removal of an Australian engineer who has been observed using swear words!' Muslims, particularly Shia, abhor swearing. Of course there was no alternative than to retain the storekeeper.

Boots wore out very quickly on the rocky surfaces and I managed to buy a very fine pair of oilman's boots with

1960 IRAN. Agha Jan Airfield. Australian, Self, Scot

protective toe caps. Some time later on another job a steel beam fell on my foot, but for the steel cap I would have lost my toes, the cap was distorted and I could not use the boots again, but what luck! We had Vickers' Vigor tractors and bulldozers for earth moving, loading, spreading fill, etc, similar to the familiar Caterpillar, but not as robust. The Vickers' had magnificent Rolls Royce engines, one of which mysteriously disintegrated, the aluminium cylinder block fell apart. The nearest Rolls Royce engineer was at Karachi, he came but was unable to explain what had occurred. Some months later I met up with the plant manager in the UK and he told me that one of his fitters, an expatriate, had decarbonised the engine by pouring in nitric acid! Christmas was approaching and my small team were hoping to be away, so after a terrific effort the runway was ready. A Dove landed just as one of our trucks was crossing over the tarmac, near heart failure all round, fortunately the pilot did not notice. Taxiing up the apron he came across and shook hands, saying, 'A fine runway.' We were very pleased. Well we finally got away on New Year's Eve, the Shell engineer agreed completion, there was a generator house to erect, we had completed the foundation and bases, the erection of the building was outside of our contract and not ready, so that was that. Off for a short leave in Amsterdam. Reporting back to head office, as there was no job currently available overseas, I accepted a posting to North Wales as agent under a project manager.

NORTH WALES 1961

Wales was a new territory for me and I found Caernarfon a delightful town, where I was to return on many occasions. The job which had barely commenced, was a factory for Ferodo, to produce brake linings, providing much needed work in an area of unemployment. The factory was so located as to be unobtrusive and with as little damaging effect on the scenery as possible. In spite of such careful planning one result when the factory was operating was a ghastly smell carried over Caernarfon, akin to burning rubber. However there had ever been a ferociously odiferous tannery in the town, so the locals got used to Ferodo, which became inevitably its name. The Ferodo representative on the project was a very capable, dedicated, cheerful and helpful individual, very interested in the work, I have forgotten but he was probably a mechanical engineer. I incurred his displeasure at the onset by erecting a large sign board on the Bangor Road, and cutting down a partially concealing hedge! Definitely not allowed. I rented a small caravan on the Menai Straits, a few hundred yards from the site, ideal accommodation. I very much enjoyed my stay there. The labour force was mainly Welsh, with a hard core of Irish. The Irish, born to the trade, deservedly well paid, hard working all hours and hard drinking. Surprisingly, to myself, expecting otherwise, the Welsh and the Irish got on famously together. My job was entirely outside supervision no office work. It rained continuously, the air warmed pleasantly by the Gulf Stream, oil skins and rubber boots, mud up to the elbows. The initial stage of the earthworks was to cut and fill in a natural valley running down to the Straits. For this we had a subcontractor using tractors and scrapers and one all powerful D9 Caterpillar Bulldozer. It was customary for major contractors to sublet much of a project. At the fill end of the site were some half dozen fully-grown oak trees which just had to go. Developers often overlook trees, a great shame, with a little thought the trees can be retained. Not discussing the problem with anyone, except the bulldozer driver, we prepared new holes at a suitable location, dug up the very large trees and carried them one by one, suspended by the bulldozer blade and replanted them. A gamble, but it was the planting season and the trees survived. Had the matter been daylighted I am sure much delay would have occurred. It was very enjoyable work, I got along well with the locals, not easy as North Wales people are not too friendly towards foreigners. I courted a young local girl, this was to have considerable bearing on my future; in consequence a short weekend in Amsterdam to say goodbye to Kufa Lily. The resident project manager, a very experienced builder, rarely left his office in the early stages and once, when he did, complained bitterly about the mud on his shoes! The visiting contracts manager I knew very well from earlier days, was a man after my own heart. He had just had a remarkable operation to lose weight, the removal of some sixteen pounds weight of fat from his abdomen, very effective but expensive on clothing. After about nine months on this job I was approached by another major contractor who worked extensively overseas. The project was to build a British bank at Tripoli, Libya. All being to my liking, I accepted and gave in my notice of leaving. The contracts manager said, 'Good luck, I am also leaving.' The chief engineer of Ferodo, who occasionally visited the site, offered me a position at their Chapel-le-Frith works, a compliment indeed, which I reluctantly turned down.

Away to London for a month of preparation and planning. A senior engineer in the firm offered me to share his flat thereby solving the temporary accommodation problem, Mounir was an Egyptian, educated at Birmingham University, highly qualified, but much more useful as a business negotiator than a performer in the field. We became great friends and still are to this day. Staff for the contract was allocated, an accountant (who was to look after the Tripoli office as well), a quantity surveyor, site engineer and a very experienced general foreman – a good team. I set off with the engineer, overland, Dover, Calais, Naples, Tripoli, taking setting-out equipment and whatever was necessary to commence the work. Various customs were curious over instrument boxes, 'Machine-guns, machine-guns,' they cried. Immigration at Tripoli was very trying but eventually we were cleared and found the Libyan Area Office, then operated by a retired Air Vice Marshal, a New Zealander who was to look after us very well in the coming years.

LIBYA 1961-63

There were few changes to Tripoli since the war years, some modern buildings and quite a bit of decay. King Idris was the ruler, a Cycenaican Senussi, he spent most of his time in Tobruk, or at Beida in the Jebel Akdar. Beida was to become the capital city of Libya, an old man's dream. I stayed at the old Del Mehari Hotel, our wartime club, cheap, comfortable enough and convenient. The head waiter, a Senussi, claimed to remember me, doubtful but nevertheless a help. The bank site was an area bounded by five roads and two buildings, the building lines right up to the roads. The main road was Sharia Istiklal, Freedom Street, the most important in Tripoli and under no circumstances could any collapse or subsidence be tolerated. Shades of the building opposite the Old Bailey in London, the Tripoli Law Courts were opposite the site! During the period in London office I had made a careful study of the deep foundation problem and had made a scale model in cardboard and balsa wood, from which the method of construction was determined. One building was a new office block, owned by the Crown Prince, the Black Prince as he was known; he passed the word that if anything happened to damage his building, there would follow dire punishment. Corrugated iron hoardings were erected, materials and plant were arriving including Larsen Sheet piling, reinforcing steel and a Ruston-Bucyrus crane with back-acter (hoe), and pile-driving equipment. For reasons best known, the customs would not release the RB and so we were stuck. One night in the early hours before dawn, I took my foreman, George, unseen by the watchmen, into the port and he drove the machine out, I going in front with a torch. Ironically, when we later tried to send it by ship to Benghazi, we had no

1961 LIBYA TRIPOLI British Bank

documents, it did not exist, so we repeated the import manoeuvre and got it away. The piling of the perimeter was very successful, George trained an Italian to operate the machine, good chap, if excitable. At one point we uncovered a 10,000 volt cable in the path of the piles. The electricity department threw up their hands in horror, impossible to move the cable. So with a crowbar, Dick, the engineer and myself levered it away the few necessary inches. A very dangerous thing to do, a catastrophe if the insulation had fractured, the delay however unacceptable. Excavation by back-acter and skip proceeded down to foundation level, the perimeter piling heavily shored with twelve inch by twelve inch timbers as the piles were exposed. At bottom we found an ancient watercourse still flowing, not a serious problem. There was, however, a very peculiar phenomenon, boils, water at high pressure bursting through the formation, fortunately easing off as though it were a safety valve. Some years later, with another company I met up with the bank manager who said that there was a flooding problem in the vaults, causing more than just inconvenience, water was entering at a joint in the retaining wall. I guessed our old friend the boils, a persistent one which had appeared after being shut away for five years. We drilled a small hole using a rock drill, inserted a one inch pipe with a tap, sealed with Sika compound. An occasional drawing off at a bucket full and that was that. Foundations, heavily reinforced concrete bases, hard work but no problems, together with the perimeter retaining walls to ground level. The concrete foundations, walls and roof were to have Tangbar steel inside the concrete. Tangbar is a flat specially malleable steel plate, supplied in lengths, to be twisted into spirals using a special machine, rendering the strongroom structures impenetrable by drill or explosive. We had the bars but the machine was not to be found, so considering that the floors were in effect one metre thick and in water, I decided to go ahead. Tangbar was, however, used in the walls and roof. The reinforced concrete frame was up to the first floor, when I was ordered to move to Beida as contracts manager for Libya.

The company had three areas of operation at that time, the bank at Tripoli, a housing programme and a maintenance contract at El Adem and Tobruk for the RAF and a very large project, housing, government offices etc. at Beida, King Idris's dream capital. I was to live at Beida where work was just beginning, a joint venture with a Cypriot contractor. The position of contracts manager was not very well considered, spread over 1,500 miles of country. Beida and Tobruk, yes, but the time consumed over Tripoli was impracticable. In fact Tobruk and El Adem being in trouble I spent most time there. Well, I married my Welsh girl in Benghazi, why I do not know, and to this day Wynn says the same. The Consul who married us, a very fine diplomat, Sir Noel Jackson, at the ceremony delivered a nice little speech about the sanctity of marriage, not to be taken lightly but with profound solemnity, very touching. After a lifetime of successful philandering I did settle down and although my wife will never believe that I have been faithful, it happens to be so. A flirtation once with her then best friend, nothing came of it, too much trouble to enter into extramarital affairs, divorce is hideous. Most people will be familiar with the incredibly pleasing exchange, most often with a complete stranger, passing in the street, a glance, a *coup d'oeil,* a secret smile, a sexual exchange. Intensely exciting, never to be forgotten, rarely repeated. Referred to sometimes as a chemical sex attraction. In this way only have I been unfaithful, but there is still a chance!

Relations with our Cypriot partners and myself were not good, too correct and straightforward in my approach to contracting, did not go down well and they contrived my removal. We moved to Benghazi, still maintaining my position as contracts manager and the appropriate salary. The job was to supervise the building of another British bank, which then was only a hole in the ground and being below the water table, flooded. To cut the story short, the building rapidly progressed, all were delighted including the architect and Mac the bank manager, who was occupying old and unsuitable premises. Mac and I were to meet many times over the years. He taught me a lot about money, investments and banking and was a very good friend to us. He came early one morning to the site, in trouble, the strong room door would not open in the old bank!

In the building trade, one inevitably learns about locks and the opening of locked doors, most carpenters are expert. It is an accomplishment never to be misused and in my experience to be carried out alone and unobserved. Without going into details, the door was opened only a little after the bank was due for business. I have been called on many occasions to break-in when keys were mislaid, sometimes when the user did not appreciate that a lock was fitted for example upside down, left hand on a right hand door, the key turning oppositely. After some months I received a letter from head office, would I return to Beida? They were not happy with the conduct of affairs there. The partner did not agree and whatever occurred, it was the end of the association. Due for leave anyway we sailed off on the *Citta di Livorno,* a pleasant trip to Catania and Naples. On board were forty beautiful horses which we assumed were going for breeding purposes,

1964 LIBYA British Bank Benghazi

we used to feed them bread and biscuits from our meals. Breeding, not so, they were unshipped at Catania, destined, we were told, for the slaughter-house and Salami. Home to Caernarfon for some leave. Reporting to London office where I was to stay a couple of months destined for a project in Saudi Arabia with the well-known Adnan Kashogi. Meanwhile a large contract in Guinea had materialized and my friend Mounir was detailed off to take charge. He came to me in a terrible state and cried, 'I cannot possibly go, what shall I do?'

I said, 'OK Mounir I will volunteer,' and straightaway saw the responsible director who agreed. Off to Paris to meet the representative of the *Société Generale,* who were the agents acting for the Guinea Government. And so back to the West Coast of Africa.

GUINEA 1963-66

Guinea consists of a mainly swampy plain rising to mountains away from the coast. Conekry is the capital and main port. Guinea borders on Guinea-Bissau and Senegal to the north, Sierra Leone and Liberia to the south and Mali, the Ivory Coast, to the east. The population consists of Fulanis and Mandingos with other smaller tribes, currently around five and a half million. Of all the West African peoples, the Guineans are by far the nicest, most colourful, well mannered and friendly. Some of the women are very beautiful, golden skinned, métisse, half-breeds. The economy is largely agricultural, now collectivised, chiefly bananas; bauxite occurs in large quantities and is developed by Harvey Aluminium of the USA, alumina is the principal export together with iron ore, all activities nationalised. Guinea was one time divided between the Gold Coast and Mali, becoming a French protectorate in the nineteenth century and later a French colony. The French way of life was very apparent, apart from the language, with men sporting berets and dangling cigarettes from their mouths in the French fashion, The British left behind in their ex-colonies a system of government, public works, etc., the French an atmosphere of *je ne sais quoi!* In 1958 France offered Guinea independence posing two questions: De Gaulle asked Sekou Touré, 'Do you wish to have independence or to remain in the French bloc, Oui ou Non?' This was probably misunderstood and Sekou Touré replied, 'Non,' ie. not to remain in the French bloc. De Gaulle's action was utterly ruthless, out with the French officials, settlers, etc., destruction of machinery and installations, destroying state records, leaving a vacuum into which the Russians and Chinese gained a foothold. Communism reigned under an absolute dictator, President Sekou Touré, who died in 1984. The army took over under Colonel Lansana. A sad story, the people of Guinea did not deserve the hardships that followed Independence; desperately short of consumer goods and a harsh regime. We had a day in Paris, very expensive it was too; catching the midnight UTA flight to Conakry, via Nouakchott in Mauritania. The airline had failed to put food and drink on board, so the very long flight, probably in a super Constellation, was miserable. Nouakchott was a god-forsaken hole, scruffy Foreign Legionnaires hanging around, bowls of coffee which were welcome. At Conakry we were met by arrangement by Spud Murphy, ex-Governor of the Gambia and then a director of the Guinean Shipping Line, looking after foreign interests in their one ship, the *Simandou,* a cargo carrier that plied between British Columbia and Japan, carrying timber, the *Simandou* had never been to Guinea. Spud became a great friend, a bachelor, who liked cooking and entertaining. We met up with Spud some years later in Cyprus, where he died suddenly. His two brothers, very distinguished Irishmen, came for the body. Waved through the customs no problem, the porters will bring your luggage! When we unpacked at the Hotel de France, our cases had been rifled, nothing of value, only small things like soap, toothpaste, toilet articles, all that was in short supply, or unobtainable in Guinea. The hotel where we were to live until our site accommodation arrived (a large caravan ex-NATO in Belgium), was a well-designed building for a hot climate, food inadequate and only Yugoslav Riesling to drink. My wife bought a small kerosene cooker and a pot and managed to feed us in the bedroom.

The foreign population was almost all diplomatic, American, British, Russian and Chinese predominating. The Russians and Chinese lived in isolation, except at ambassador level there was no outside contact. The Russians mostly engaged in trade, goods in exchange for bananas was a favourite and of course politics. Soon after we started operating, Sekou Touré threw the Russians out, too much interference in Guinea's affairs. The Chinese were building a cigarette factory and a cultural centre. They used almost no machinery, all hand labour, Chinese only, but of course produced very elegant results. The *Complexe Textile* project consisted of 700 looms spinning, weaving, dyeing and printing plant, with ancillary services and staff housing. The scheme a masterpiece of financial negotiation, was set up between *Société Generale* and Platts, the textile machinery manufacturers; some cotton was available in Guinea, but the bulk was to be imported. We had our own architectural, structural engineering, mechanical and electrical design departments, as did most other major contractors, a comfortable arrangement which eased the frequently difficult relationships vis-à-vis architect-contractor, but made for a satisfactory result. It did, however, entail more responsibility for the man on the site who was encouraged to iron out problems on his own initiative. I went out to the site on arrival, easily found, forty miles from Conakry and overlooked by a prominent mountain peak, Kakolima, le chien qui fume, supposedly once volcanic; our area flat, barren ironstone fringed with thin bush, few trees, one very large prominent mango tree. Early morning I got out of the car and dropping my shorts, squatted to do my business, a movement alerted me to a creature similarly performing, a beautiful animal of the wild cat family, we called them, mistakenly, jaguars, never discovered their species, silky black, about three feet long, golden eyes. (The puma or cougar fit the description, but are said to be South American, reddish-brown in colour.) We looked at each other and fortunately parted peacefully; there was one that used to tramp about on our caravan roof at night and when disturbed would leap gracefully down into the valley many feet below. The big animals had gone up country, baboons and monkeys abounded around the site and of course snakes galore. An ex-Guards officer, a remittance man we thought, very handsome, charming and physically attractive, was hunting crocodiles in a nearby river, the belly skin sold at something in the region of £1 a square inch. He

1964 GUINEA. Textile complex Kakolima mountain.

1965 GUINEA. Textile complex

always stopped off for a drink at our dwelling.

The build-up was very rapid, the company shipping department was very efficient, soon we were living on site, the perimeter fence established and setting out of buildings finalised. A prominent Lebanese contractor had just completed a major water-pipeline installation and had available all necessary staff and labour, so by arrangement between our respective head offices, they took over the bulk of the construction under our supervision. The caravan is worth a description: US made, thirty feet long, double axle, corner jacks, bought second-hand from NATO, perfectly adequate housing for three years, divided into double-bunk room, (we used as a store), shower and toilet, kitchen, sitting-dining, double bedroom. Services were water tanker, electricity generator and septic tank. All very cosy provided one was tidy. For food, etc., we imported from a specialist firm in the UK, in our case duty free. One could only order in bulk; one time we ended up with twelve cases of Edam cheese and twelve by twelve cases of Calvados! In an attractive situation we had many visitors and made many friends, mainly diplomatic, British, American and German, some to this day we correspond with. The factory, roughly the floor area in size of eight football pitches, required the ironstone to be blasted down to a level about one metre below existing ground. An area was drilled at one metre spacings and I decided to use two sticks of dynamite per hole. We stood under the great mango tree and bang, the result was devastating, rocks going high up in the air and showering down on the tree. Our adoptive tame monkey, Paris, ran off, never to return. Afterwards one stick per hole proved the right amount. All went very well with the construction, a very successful operation, everyone working all hours, little else to do, the odd trip to Freetown to see the dentist, or for some items unobtainable in Guinea.

My key staff were obliged to leave after about one year. The accountant, a staunch Catholic with seven children and another just born, had to go home to his wife. A very likeable man, our tamed wild cat loved him, would sit on his knee and delicately sniff at his armpit, unremarked by us and he did not seem to realize his hidden attraction!. The surveyor had been some twelve years on the Coast and was going blind from the side effect of Mepacrine, anti-malaria pills, so he had to go. It was decided not to replace them, I would feed them with the necessary facts and figures to enable the paper work to be done in London. This entailed a great deal of work, very long hours each day. I recruited Wynn to assist in the collection of the material and to do the vast amount of typing involved. She was suitably recompensed. To this day she swears she never received anything, in a sense true, because whatever she earned went into my account, which was hers anyway! On top of all this I had a bad accident, in the blinding monsoon rain I slipped on the wet concrete floor, trapping my leg in a small pipe duct. The resulting embolism, huge clot of blood on my calf muscle, was horrendous. The British Ambassador's wife, we knew, was a doctor. She said, 'But I have never practised, as soon as I qualified, I married. However,' she said, 'the *Hope Ship* is arriving now, you can see a doctor on board.' (There were no medical facilities in Guinea! The *Hope Ship*, American, cruised the Third World countries treating the sick and teaching simple remedies, a truly beneficial venture. Queuing up with hundreds of Africans (no racism here), I finally got to see a surgeon, a well-known New York specialist, who without anaesthetic opened up the clot with a table knife and spooned out masses of black goo. He explained that they practised the most primitive methods, in reach of the people themselves. Twice daily, hot salt water soaks in a bucket was the treatment for the wound, a great hole, made worse by an old bullet wound in the same area. Dressings were a problem, we exhausted the bed sheets and it was necessary to have prepared dressings flown out. It never healed up until returning to the UK. The monsoon rains and storms were stupendous, as much rain would fall in one day as, say, Manchester received in a year – around thirty inches! Visibility was often reduced to nil and our road to the coast washed out. We would go out at night to shower in the rain; on one occasion we were caught in a waterspout which caused, not cats and dogs, but small animals such as frogs, lizards and grass snakes to descend on and around us, ice cold to the touch. The factory gutters, large rectangular troughs, ran full to overflowing and it was necessary to increase the slopes. Lightning bounced spectacularly off the ironstone, an awesome display of power. Due to a political disagreement with Britain, the nature of which I have forgotten, the

The British Embassy staff leaving after the breaking off of diplomatic relations

Ambassador and his staff left or were asked to leave. Sad to see our friends go, we were put under the protection of the American Embassy, equally well-known to us. We organized a safari to a river not too far up country, to see the hippos, with our American friends and dear Spud Murphy. It was necessary to spend the night in order to observe the hippos at dawn, which we did. Unforgettably we saw Spud, in the starlight, get up from his camp bed, put on a clean white shirt, cuff-links, studs and tie, dressed as for the office!

With a lovely, blonde embassy girl, Nancy, and the crocodile hunter, we climbed Kakolima, very hard going, did not do my leg much good. The baboons, unseen, but very noisy, were said to be dangerous and in fact it was nerve-racking. Nancy was one of the most delectable females we ever met, given to wearing the shortest shorts over such perfect curves. She was making a play for the hunter, no dice! In due course the mill commenced operating, the expatriate staff, mostly Lancashire born, had been together in the Phillipines. They were a very jolly crowd and expert at their jobs. The Minister for Economy came to see the factory working, introduced to him he said, 'Ah the always immaculately dressed engineer with one white leg,' (my bandages)! A good time to go on leave, the company were very generous doubling my leave entitlement which meant ten month's pay. We only took two months and returned for the defects, maintenance and handover period. This time we travelled KLM from Amsterdam, which ran a service down the coast. Conakry was blacked out by a storm so the plane overshot and landed in Liberia at Monrovia, the American-favoured state, created for the settlement of ex slaves. Fortunately we had an old friend there, the Caterpillar Tractor Agent, who made our enforced three days' stay enjoyable. We were absolutely dumbfounded by his arrogant treatment of the Liberians, particularly as they were extremely sensitive. A few days previously a BOAC and a KLM pilot had been publicly flogged for insulting President Tupman and here was our friend Bill behaving like Hitler.

We had disposed of the site accommodation but there was no problem, so many people going on leave looking for caretakers. We looked after the CIA Chief's house and then the KLM manager's, outside Conakry and conveniently on the way to the mill, spending only a short time in a new, very crummy Yugoslav built hotel. All went well and the completion certificate was issued. There being at the time no work overseas, there followed several months, not unpleasant to rediscover London, spent at head office, investigating and planning possible future contracts. During this time the Chairman and Founder, Sir Richard died and a funeral service was held at Westminster Abbey. Several directors were waiting in a company Rolls Royce for the chauffeur, who had disappeared. Would I drive them? Stopping the car at the Abbey gates, my passengers alighted, I pressed the starter, no response! The policeman at the gate became very excited, we all have noticed this often wondering why a policeman of any nationality, gets so frantic when controlling traffic, to the point of apoplexy. The chauffeur of the following Rolls came up and reaching under the dash flipped a switch, an anti-theft device, saying, 'Well, you wouldn't know about this.'

Of course working overseas for different contractors opens the door and other approaches were made during the period, which I resisted having a good relationship with the late Sir Richard's organization. However, I finally succumbed to an offer from a construction company based in Wolverhampton, who required a general manager to establish a new company in Libya. Interviewed by the board of directors, I posed the question, 'Why do you want to open up in Libya? Contracting is very difficult there and in spite of oil wealth, there are not so many opportunities.' Well they were partners in the North Sea with an American oil company, who were also operating in Libya. In addition the chosen Libyan 'sleeping partner', a minister in government, was expected to be more than useful. In the event the oil company was, shall we say, only sympathetic and the minister a non-runner.

LIBYA 1966-67

Off we went by road to Naples and the familiar Italian *Citta di Livorno,* in a new Austin 1800, loaded to the gills. At Dover the Customs, checking the log book, discovered that it was for an identical model but recording the wrong chassis and engine numbers. The Customs' officer said, 'What do you want to do? Go on?'

'Yes,' I replied, and did

At Tripoli the usual 'Machine-guns, machine-guns!' None, but they did spot the incorrect paperwork and refused to let the car in! For a week I pestered the Customs' chief who at last in exasperation said, 'I am fed up with you, go away and take your car.' The said car was a great disappointment, continually breaking down. I listed eighteen faults in the nine months we used it, the foreman of the BMC agent's garage, an Italian, would throw up his arms in despair when it appeared. If I remember correctly, it was necessary to remove the engine to replace the fanbelt, but perhaps I exaggerate. BMC at one stage did publish an apology of sorts. They had distributed the model without the three or four years' development period. Additionally, I was not pleased at a considerable loss when British Leyland were nationalized, I had 5,620 shares purchased at twenty-one shillings, deciding the shares were not worth keeping, as it turned out, rightly so, I sold them for the miserable sum of two shillings each. Beware of reversal to recent privatisation, something quite similar could happen. I had a very experienced estimator and we tendered for several major and medium building, or civil engineering works. On every occasion we were the highest bidders, not because of caution, but simply that others put in ridiculously low prices, probably knowing that they could manipulate the authorities to up the ante, as the work progressed, which we certainly could not count on. My old friend Mac the bank manager was then based in Tripoli and it was then that the incident occurred with the flooded vaults. We were to cross paths with Mac in Jordan and again in Cyprus. Two directors visited after we had been 'inoperative' for some months and decided to wind up the company. The venture cost little since the monies deposited as development capital was untouched. Coincidental with this decision, the company had won a large contract in Jordan, the King Hussein Military 650 bed hospital complex and I accepted the offer to go as project manager. This was then early 1967. Changing airlines in Cairo we lost all our baggage, fortunately insured. In Tripoli we had packed everything including the furniture, routed to the port of Aqaba.

There was no market at all the for miserable aforementioned car, so I shipped it back to the UK, much to the annoyance of the company, who would have been equally cross if it were to have been abandoned. The hospital was a joint venture with a Jordanian company, who were in fact essentially Palestinians, homeless and embittered, particularly of course against the Israelis, but also against the British because of the 1917 Balfour declaration and the UN partition of Palestine in 1948, for which they also blamed the British. A very unhappy people, not the easiest to live and work with. We knew very few actual Jordanians, the future Prime Minister for one and another the man who collected the rubbish.

JORDAN 1967-1970

The Hashemite Kingdom of Jordan is land-locked, except for an outlet on the Red Sea at Aqaba; mainly desert but quite fertile towards the west, and the north, Syria. The people are Arab, Sunni Muslims with Christians and others. Phosphates are the principal export as fertilisers; tourism is the mainstay of the economy. Agriculture is concentrated in the fertile Jordan Valley. We enjoyed the best quality and variety of fruit and vegetables, unequalled in our experience elsewhere. There is a little copper mined, no oil and one suspects that in such likely desert country oil does exist but presumably the risks in getting it out are not worth the costs of exploration.

There is evidence that Jordan flourished in the Bronze Age and was part of the Roman Empire about the same time as Britain, 60 BC. Through the centuries it was controlled by Arabs and Turks, the Crusaders intervening in the eleventh and twelfth centuries. In 1917, during the Great War, the Turks were expelled and a mandate established under British control, when the country was known as Transjordan. I well remember as a boy, stories of the colourful Transjordan Frontier Force. In 1946 it became an independent Kingdom, named Jordan. In the Arab-Israeli War of 1948-49 Jordan overran the West Bank of the River Jordan including part of the City of Jerusalem, subsequently regained by Israel in the 1967 War. Israel has since been criticised frequently for not setting up a self-governing state for the Palestinians. The PLO carried out many raids across the East Bank; they were, however, subdued by Jordanian forces in the Civil War of 1970-71. The Civil War was very vicious, we lost much time on the job; King Hussein's élite Bedouin Soldiers finally overthrew the PLO force, who left for the Lebanon to continue operations against Israel from there. The population currently is around three and a half million, including the West Bank. Jordan is most attractive for tourists, Petra, the Red Rose City, we enjoyed very much, the Chinese Silk Road passed through there in Nabattean times, travelled once by Marco Polo en route to China. Ctesiphon, mentioned on the Kut Road was also on this 4,000 miles route. Jerash of Roman antiquity is also very interesting, as is the Philladelphia stadium in Amman. Karl Marx wrote:

> History teaches us that conflict is the motive force of life.

Well, I had already seen enough and now we were to be embroiled in the June 1967 Arab-Israeli War, known as the Six Day War. Towards the end of May, feelings were running high in Amman, throw the Jews into the sea, down with the British and Americans; we were advised not to go into the town. On site, where work had commenced, I was obliged to go home. We were told by our partners to leave our temporary flat and move into the Intercontinental Hotel, for safety. They were not very friendly and did nothing to help us. That same day from the hotel we watched the bombing of Amman airport, the Israeli planes dropped penetration bombs which successfully cratered the runway. Pandemonium broke out all round, guests were ordered down to shelter in the basement, a cook ran amok among us with a carving knife, but was restrained, causing no harm. There was no service for two or three days, but with the small group we had gathered we managed to scrounge some bits and pieces. My wife and I went out into a nearby street, deserted and very eerie, and from a small shop acquired some whisky, fruit and above all batteries for our radio; we had absolutely no news of what was happening. However, the batteries did not help, we could not raise the BBC and at such a critical time! In the next room to ours was a very well-known PLO leader, no names, with his Egyptian girlfriend and three bodyguards. After some days they left and we understood that the girl was put to washing dishes in the kitchens. We saw very disconsolate soldiers coming back from the fighting, probably deserters. There were air-raid alerts but no action. The British Ambassador addressed us and advised that all foreigners should leave, an evacuation was planned for the following day by the USAF, coaches would leave in the very early hours to avoid interference. Around dawn at the airport, the runway had been temporarily repaired, fourteen C130 USAF transport planes landed, the first disgorging a number of 'civilians', who rapidly organized the embarkation of some 1,500 persons each carrying a minimum of possessions. A remarkable achievement, the C130's engines had not been shut down and the whole circus took off in line ahead, all in about fifteen minutes, bound as we learned later for Tehran. On our plane was a well-known TV journalist and commentator, we had a bottle of whisky and he had a tin of bully beef, which we shared. We met up with him again at Heathrow where he was covering a serious dispute between Arab and Israeli airline staffs. Arriving at Beirut Airport the day after the Israelis had destroyed seven airlines on the ground, he popped up again, greeting us with, 'You two again, trouble wherever you go!' A passenger was mysteriously poking a baby's feeding bottle into a zip bag, he reluctantly showed us a baby chihuahua, its little head coming up to look around. We took off the following day from Tehran to Gatwick by RAF Hastings, seats facing to the rear, most peculiar. Well the US airforce ride was free, the RAF charged £240 each. After a couple of weeks it was considered safe to return and I went back alone. The atmosphere was very tense. Naturally our friends were shattered by the swiftness of the Israeli strike and the occupation of the West Bank. There was time for me to complete the plan for the execution of the works, a very satisfactory scheme as it turned out. There was a large expatriate staff involved together with an equal number of Palestinian engineers, accountants, foremen, etc., and a labour force of around one thousand. It all went very well, a satisfactory project. Work was not infrequently halted by the appearance of Israeli fighter planes. The Israelis attacked in force across the Jordan valley at Karami, in reprisal for raids by the PLO. We could follow the progress of the fight quite clearly, below us in the valley. The Israelis were repelled and thrown back by the Jordanian army, a heartening victory for the poor beset Kingdom.

The civil war flared up frequently, very intense, finally to be settled in 1971 by the expulsion of the militant Palestinians to the Lebanon. Many disturbing incidents including robbery and rape occurred during these troubles. For self-protection I acquired a very nice 9 mm Czech pistol, which I taught my wife to use and to keep it handy at home, fortunately fired once only for practice. We made very good, lasting friends in Jordan and on our days off took to the countryside, very pleasantly wooded to the north of Amman. We were arrested

1968 JORDAN. King Hussein Military Hospital ward blocks

1968 JORDAN. The Mosque

1969 JORDAN. King Hussein Military Hospital entrance

by a group of guerillas one time and driven for miles to their camp overlooking the Dead Sea. The officer in charge was a previous employee we knew well, so it ended in a feast in the desert. The consultants for the design of the project were originally a well-known British group, who for reasons best known were superseded by a Swedish consultant of international repute, who continued the design details, which in the event were far from complete. Their comparatively young engineer on site, a sterling character, poor chap, was overwhelmed with work. Against some opposition I decided to help him out, after all it would have been useless to let things grind down, no help to anyone. So altogether I made some 1,400 drawings, sketches, design notes, instructions, etc., certainly in the final settlement the company was reimbursed and I did receive a reasonable bonus. Accidents are common on building sites, only one fatality there, a very likeable young water-tanker driver collided with a 450 volt temporary powerline and stepping down from the vehicle, earthed himself to death. Electrical accidents are most prevalent. A very common accident is stepping on a board with a protruding nail, painful; the treatment, pull the board off the foot, or vice versa, bang with a piece of wood and cauterise with a cigarette end. This happened to myself and twenty years later an operation became necessary to remove the, until then, concealed debris.

The company had agreed to build a mosque free of cost, the location was marked on the site plan but no details. I adopted the construction of the mosque as my baby. To find out the requirements was pure detective work, piece by piece; orientation towards Mecca, understood; I worked out a compass bearing from a small atlas and that established the axis of the building. Toilets and washing facilities in the basement, the whole row of urinals each with water tap; steel windows with grills, to prevent the theft of valuable carpets, I was informed; the brass crescent symbols, made in Beirut, for dome and minaret; the best quality Carrara marble floor. The dome was made of plastic in four bolted sections, to my design, by a firm in England, looked splendid in its shiny green facing. The special iron stairs inside the minaret required very careful calculation to arrive exactly at the landing in even risers.

Roman ruins – many remain in Jordan

The climate in Amman was very pleasant, not too hot in summer, cold but invigorating winters. In the winter of 1969, King Hussein was to lay the foundation stone; the stone beautifully sculpted; (Jordanian stonemasons are among the best,) all ready for the great day. Overnight it snowed heavily, as much as two metres deep in drifts, quite normal for Amman but never lasted long. With much difficulty I drove to the site (my car then a first-class Chevrolet), and arrived with General Majali, Chief of the Medical Corps; none other arrived. We looked at each other and grinned. I pointed out he was minus a button on his greatcoat, we shared a thermos of coffee my wife had provided and home we went. Towards the end of the job my wife fell on the newly washed marble stairs, broke her leg and was flown home; on the plane she spotted that a man sitting next to her was wearing a revolver in a shoulder holster. He saw she had noticed and said, 'Don't worry my dear, I am the security guard!' I joined her in Wales and we had an enjoyable leave, making plans for a tentative retirement. A bit early one may think, but generally work in difficult climatic conditions counted as twenty-five per cent more timewise, so that normal retirement age could reasonably be between fifty-five to sixty years. Not a bad idea, bearing in mind that not long ago men retired at sixty-five and the expectation of life was one year only! My father retired at fifty-eight and lived a good life until seventy-six. Pneumonia, known as the old man's friend had by then been successfully dealt with, of course more less friendly illnesses became prevalent. However out of the blue came an offer to manage the construction of a Hilton Hotel in Abu Dhabi then a sheikhdom under the Ruler, Sheikh Zayed bin Sultan al-Nahayan, for whom the project was being built; Hilton do not own anything, similar to Royal Dutch Petroleum, they manage and operate under their name. So there we were back to the Gulf, dreadful climate, ameliorated these days by air-conditioning and adequate water supplies.

ABU DHABI 1970-1973

One of the several Sheikhdoms, along the southern side of the Gulf, opposite Iran, Abu Dhabi in 1820 entered into treaties with Britain, the Royal Navy being very active in the Gulf since that time, particularly of course during the Iran-Iraq conflict. In 1890 Britain established Protectorates which survived until the Federation of the seven Sheikhdoms in 1971, the United Arab Emirates, with Sheikh Zayed as the overall Ruler and Abu Dhabi as the capital. The UAE consists of the Sheikhdoms of Abu Dhabi, Ajman, Dubai, Fujairah, Ras Al Khaimah, Sharjah and Um Al Qaiwan, Abu Dhabi comprises eighty-five per cent of the land area and with Dubai, one third of the population. The capital, Abu Dhabi, is a small island, separated from the mainland by a bridge over a narrow seaway, flat sandy desert, barren except where fully grown trees have been imported and planted at great expense. Oil is produced in great quantities both underground and off shore, the resulting riches have produced in Abu Dhabi and Dubai, modern airports, ports, desalination plants, etc. *Per capita* UAE is the richest in the world; children were paid to attend school; the Abu Dhabians do not work except in the forces, the government and are also presumably by choice, drivers. Health services are free; professional activities were mainly carried out then by Egyptians. The total population is about one and a third million Arabs of Sunni Muslim persuasion. UAE is a prominent member of OPEC. The defence force was then officered by British Army seconded or contract personnel, we had many serving friends. In some ways it was a survival of the old Indian Army, the last of the Raj. At the HQ mess on party nights, two mounted lancers were hoisted up on top of the entrance gate towers, with illuminations, pure Hollywood. The small airforce comprised Hunter fighters and helicopters, very competently flown by carefully selected RAF pilots; a compatriot of my wife, Dai Jones did not survive, putting his Hunter into the ground! The small, effective navy was equipped with fast, heavily-armed patrol boats, very dashing.

We had many old friends in Dubai and Sharjah, ex the Libyan banks, a fairly short drive across the desert; the fort at Sharjah was a staging post for Imperial Airways going back to the early twenties, we stayed there with friends from Cable and Wireless whose HQ it became. I met Sheikh Zayed only once, in the middle of the night, as was his custom, at a palace miles out in the desert, the reception room sparsely, albeit expensively, furnished in the traditional Bedouin manner. I had been warned not to mention such projects as a staircase to the moon, a joke, but the ruler might say, 'Right, I will have one!' The proposal for a roof garden on the hotel he did not accept however, too expensive he considered. The sand on the island was particularly unstable, in the palm of the hand grains would roll about like ball-bearings. Containment as was used on the Kufa-Nejaf road is the usual method of stabilisation, however the company had a subsidiary in Bombay specialising in piling (Bombay is practically built on piles), also employing a process called Vibroflot which it was planned to use on the foundations. The system consists of a twenty feet long, say twelve inch diameter steel vibrating poker, supported by a crane with a constant supply of fresh water passing through the head. The poker is vibrated down to its full length and slowly withdrawn whilst still vibrating. The resulting area, over some four to five feet in diameter, is perfectly firm and remains so. The Vibroflot equipment and a team were quickly shipped from Bombay with a very competent Indian engineer. The Indians were a delight to work with, quiet and unobtrusive in their work. Coming from a somewhat restricted economy they were overjoyed to receive some beer, cigarettes etc., and a little spending money. Abu Dhabi was dry but foreigners had a monthly allowance, graduated according to their position, so I had some to spare. Our bungalow was most impressive, having been decorated and furnished with spare materials from one of the many palaces. Fully air-conditioned, essential for eight months of the year, it was so humid outside that twice my sunglasses shattered going out. We found a window forced one morning and called the police, the sergeant said, 'Don't worry, we shot him coming from your house.' The labour used on the project was mainly Pakistani, some Indian, nearly all 'boat people', illegal immigrants from Karachi and Bombay by launches, overcrowded, unsafe and often many passengers lost at sea.

Splendid craftsmen, I remembered stories of their tribesmen being capable of turning out Lee Enfield rifles by hand, except for the bolts, which they had to steal (throwing the bolts away at Dunkirk and discarding the rifles!) The building externally not exciting, but internally exceedingly

1970-73 ABU DHABI Hilton

1971 ABU DHABI. French made armoured car

beautiful, the design and decor by an American interior designer based in Athens. The architect asked to provide a picture window wall in the bar, refused; I have always remembered him saying, 'You look inwards.'

The lounges, restaurants, bars etc., were splendidly appointed. At the end I spent sometime with the Hilton housekeeper placing the furniture and paintings room by room, all to the designer's drawings; mysteriously cushions would vanish, to be found in bedrooms. Very exciting when the hotel was in use, many snags all put right in the end.

Expatriate staff were the usual problem, never content with their lot, ever dissatisfied; well paid and housed and after all, there of their own choice. A not unamusing incident with an excellent painting supervisor, he became maniac and had to be repatriated. His successor, equally expert, turned out to be an alcoholic and he went. Only one fatal accident, an electrician using a breast drill against his bare sweaty chest was electrocuted. Over the years I have several times had to appear in court in such cases. The manager is very much responsible to the law and is blamed entirely by the labour force. Logically there is no such thing as an accident, there is a reason and a cause for any injury; the knife does not 'accidentally' cut your finger, you introduce your digit in front of the cutting edge. One such incident in Ghana saw me, suit and tie sweating profusely, the Judge a great obese black man, one witness obviously drunk! The Judge, 'You, that black man, you be drunk, how you dare, out my court.' The climax, to the accused person in the dock. Very severely – the Judge, 'I am going to imprison you for life, I am going to hang you,' fined £5. Ironically I paid the fine. A Swiss friend working in China as manager of a factory producing aluminium wares told me that always in the case of inevitable injuries to the workmen, he was automatically fined. He designed a series of large posters, for example, a man striking his thumb with a hammer and a suitable exclamation, to convince the authorities that he had given sufficient warning. Of course he was still fined. Well, we thought enough was enough and planned to retire after Abu Dhabi, arranging our finances for this event, over the preceding year, with the kind help of our bank friends. Pensions do not come early except for certain classes of overseas employment, government service, banks, commercial, but not the mobile, contractor's man. One is well paid, often without income tax deduction and on changing employers can receive all or part of one's contributions. As an example however, for loyal service over quite a few years I receive a pension of £2.30 per week after tax and never increased over a period of several years.

7

OUT TO GRASS

Retirement is quite shattering, giving up controlled active life to a situation where you are on your own, starting again from scratch. Much advice has been given on how to have a happy ending. Two examples came frequently to mind, my father, minor civil servant, considered that he had wasted his working years, in those times it was a safe job and the dangling carrot, a small pension. So disillusioned, he retired before sixty and lived comfortably beyond the allotted span, active with the garden, his small workshop and the endless make, mend and decoration of a house. No money problems – very important for peace of mind. His brother, my uncle, took another road; he spent his working life at the Public Records' Office, then at Somerset House, also retiring early on. Early retirement was essential then if you wanted to live beyond sixty-six years it seems, the then expectation of life. My uncle led a sedentary life, doing no work whatsoever, dressed very carefully, strolled to the library, rested and read, a game of bridge, passing the time in a completely leisurely fashion. He lived to what was then considered to be a ripe old age.

We had planned to stay in the Lebanon, a country we had enjoyed on several occasions and where we had many acquaintances. A furnished, rented apartment on the seafront at Beirut was admirable, unfortunately it was not far from a Palestinian Refugee camp, which was often attacked. We looked at several houses over a period of about three months and finally settled on a very nice dwelling in the hills at Juni. About this time the Israelis were constantly bombing the nearby camp and there were frequent curfews. When we met finally at the lawyer's office to conclude the purchase of the

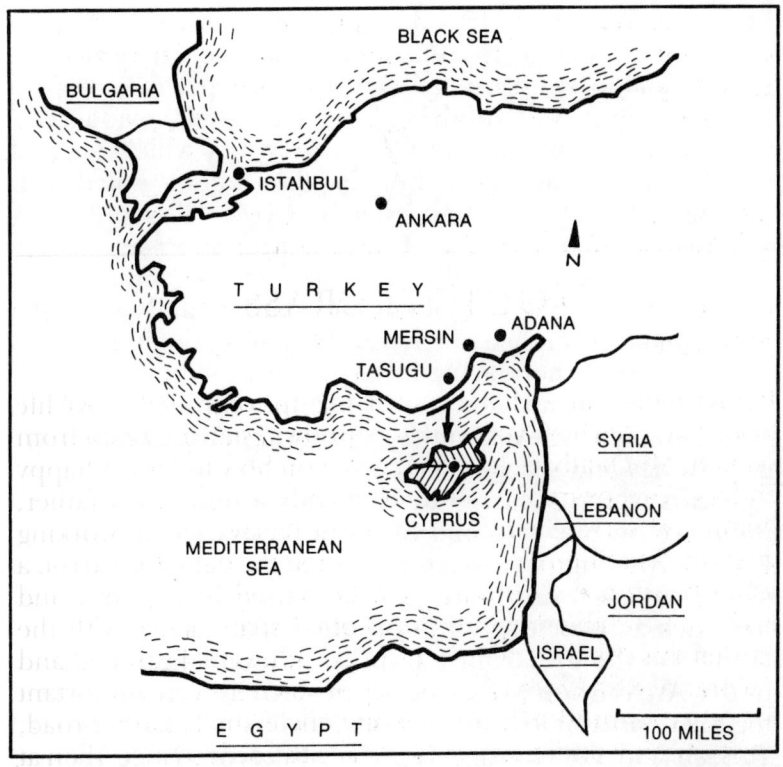

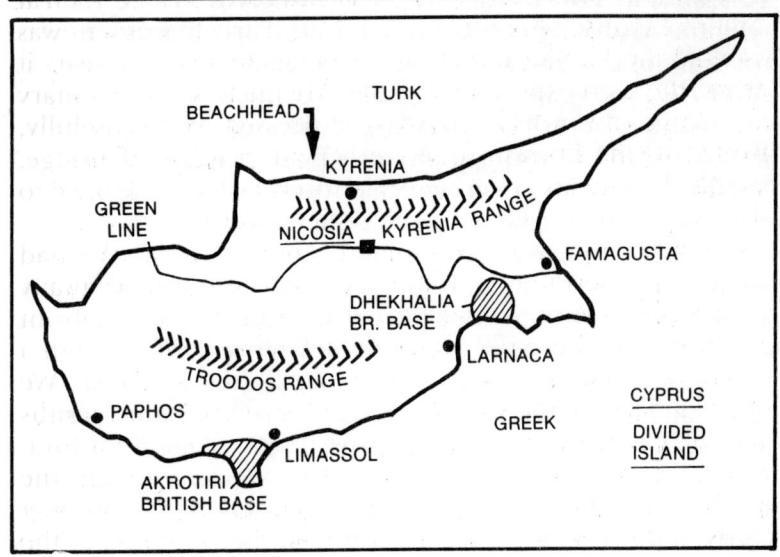

Map 1: Eastern Mediterranean region showing Bulgaria, Turkey (with Istanbul, Ankara, Mersin, Tasugu, Adana), Cyprus, Syria, Lebanon, Jordan, Israel, and Egypt. Scale: 100 miles.

Map 2: Cyprus – Divided Island, showing the Turkish beachhead at Kyrenia, the Green Line, Nicosia, Kyrenia Range, Famagusta, Dhekhalia British Base, Larnaca, Troodos Range, Paphos, Limassol, and Akrotiri British Base.

house, the lawyer, my friend for life ever after, said, 'Why do you want to stay in Beirut? In any case you may not get presidential permission to take up residence!' At such a forthright hint, we withdrew from the sale. Providence, I wonder! Overnight we decided on Cyprus which we had visited several times and in a few days off we sailed, car, baggage and all. The best spot in Cyprus was obviously Kyrenia. So there we went. Houses were in short supply and we were in a hurry to settle, so in a few days we found a very nice flat in a small development, with gardens and swimming pool, not far from the sea anyway. We had a good time in '73 and part of '74, holidaying in Europe, travelling extensively round the island, money plentiful, activities galore, swimming, eating well and especially drinking inexpensive good wines and spirits.

Events which occurred in 1974 were to have a profound influence on our lives and of many thousands of others in Cyprus. Although free to move, we remained, undecided over where to go. It is worthwhile to look at the major incident that had such an upsetting effect on our retirement.

In 1958 the British gave Cyprus, a colony, independence under Archbishop Makarios. Up to 1963 the Cypriots lived together, more or less, in harmony, surprisingly since those of Turkish and Greek origin were of different ethnic groups, religions and languages. Until we lived in Cyprus we were unaware of the divide; Cypriots appeared to be one people. After 1964 there was considerable dissention between the two camps, 'massacres' occurred, mainly among village communities. This led to a segregation into separate villages, zones and satellites, virtually a piecemeal division of the island. The central plain became entirely Turkish and Greek Cypriots could only pass in convoys controlled by a UN force, the latter having appeared on the scene as peacekeepers, where as UNFICYP they have operated ever since. The UN also established a chain of observation posts in towns and villages, to prevent intersectarian strife. Sometimes murders took place on both sides. The differences were highlighted by the wide display of Greek and Turkish flags. General Grivas, a Greek officer, a colourful personality, led an underground movement, EOKA, seeking *ENOSIS,* union with Greece, very much a thorn in the side of the British before 1958. Under

Makarios the National Guard was formed, the official Cyprus government armed force. The Turks had a 'private' militia, which in the event proved to be well-armed and organized. In July 1974, a right-wing politician, Samson, organized a coup against the government and ousted Makarios. We were actually on holiday in Paphos and witnessed the Archbishop leaving by helicopter from the police HQ yard. It became obvious, especially to the Turks, that genocide was about to take place. Turkey, Greece and Britain were the guarantor powers of the sovereignty of Cyprus, so Ecevit, Foreign Secretary of Turkey, went to see Callaghan, his opposite number in Britain, to enquire what Britain was going to do? Ecevit went away with no proper response, although there was a crack force of some 7,000 troops in the British sovereign bases and a UN peace keeping force of around 13,000 all heavily armed and equipped, with only a meagre National Guard to contain. What happened was inevitable, the only possible solution in the circumstances, not a happy one; a divided small island. The National Guard, Greek officered and trained, was mainly armed with Egypt's left-overs from the 1967 Arab-Israeli War, of USSR origin including a few T54 tanks (all of which had proved inadequate against the Israelis), no artillery, no air, primitive AA guns. The Turkish militia had small arms only. There is a museum of captured Greek weapons near the invasion beach, rather pathetic, but in fact the National Guard fought well. The mainland Turks were of course well-equipped; destroyers, M60 tanks, landing craft, and a formidable air force as supplied by USA to a NATO ally. At dawn, 05.00 on 20 July 1974, we were awakened by bombing close at hand. We fell out of bed to the floor and looking out, saw Phantom jets dive-bombing National Guard positions around us and on the outskirts of Kyrenia, one could see the silvery bombs falling through the air. Off the coast the invasion fleet approached covered by three destroyers, firing on the area immediately behind the coast road and into the foothills. Later in the morning many small helicopters passed overhead carrying airborne troops obviously destined for the Nicosia area, to contain the National Guard; we counted around eighty at one time. Hannibals and Hercules transport planes followed, carrying paratroops. The Phantoms were active in the south and

1974 CYPRUS. Turkish memorial

against the northern foothills. There was some firing from the beach-head some five miles from us; shelling by the destroyers at Greek concentrations in the foothills; the tanks we could hear, roaring away down the Kyrenia-Nicosia road and along the coast road east and west. We generally stayed out of doors (on the west perimeter of Kyrenia), watching the fun, not so funny later on.

That night, with neighbours, we gathered together on the ground floor, placing mattresses against the windows; a Greek judge, wife and son; an American ex-diplomat and wife; an American Quaker, who drove an ambulance in the Second World War and I swear picked me up from the back of my tank in the Western desert; two Greek families; two English holiday families.

Wars usually quieten down at dusk and we spent a peaceful night. Water and electricity were off, but we had small roof water tanks.

The next day, of course, the seasonal hot weather, fine as

usual, the Greek judge decided to make a run for Nicosia, as his car was short of petrol, some was syphoned from mine by an obliging Greek soldier. During the day the Greek and some English families moved to a large coastal hotel in the middle of Kyrenia, where many refugees gathered, along with evacuees from adjacent villages. The fighting around us increased and we were obliged to take shelter under the stairs, fortunately roomy and of concrete construction. There in fact we spent several days and nights, only sallying out for food and water.

During the period the Greek soldiers withdrew from our location (taking my binoculars!) and activity spread from the landing area to clean up the surrounding areas and into the foothills. About the fourth day, really very quiet with only occasional MG and rifle fire, the Turks began to infiltrate over the area with killings of civilians sheltering in houses. The next morning my wife and I and the Quaker decided to move to the Turkish quarter of Kyrenia where we should be safe. In both our cars we drove slowly to the area of the hotel when he decided he had to return for some papers. Whilst we waited, surrounded by wounded Greek soldiers, mostly burns, (probably not napalm, rather forest fires), a small Royal Navy helicopter landed in the hotel car park. A naval officer

HMS *Liverpool* missile cruiser

Source unknown

dismounted and said, 'What on earth are you doing here? Get aboard,' which we did, carrying only a bagful of water. The helicopter landed on the aircraft carrier HMS *Hermes*, we the last arrivals. We were given the engineer captain's cabin! The *Hermes* sailed along the east and the south coast. In the night we were transferred by helicopter to the missile cruiser HMS *Liverpool* and the following night by helicopter to the UK sovereign base at Dhaklia. Then, and later, I was very impressed by the superiority of the soldiers and sailors we met. And so kind. After two or three days a friend, the general manager of Shell, learned we were in Dhaklia and 'rescued' us, driving us to his home, Shell House, on the northern outskirts of Nicosia, comparatively quiet. We could follow the progress of the Turks, clearing pockets of Greeks towards us across the central plain.

It turned out that we had run into a hornet's nest, the Turks advanced day by day and for four horrible days we were pinned down in the cellar, with fighting raging overhead. Constant bombing by the Phantoms and incessant MG and rifle fire. This lasted for four days and the final night the Turks took us over, very anxious civilians. Fortunately the officer in charge knew us, he was a schoolmaster from Kyrenia, what luck! We watched the National Guard remnants funnel back into the streets of Nicosia and it was over. The Turks halted on what became the Green Line.

I returned to our home in Kyrenia, escorted by police. One indescribable mess, looted and desecrated beyond belief, no water, no electricity, the stench of death, unburied soldiers. My car was where I had left it and I had the keys, so with few possessions returned to Shell House for a month until the situation returned to some normality.

In 1975 the Turkish population in the south were ordered to move to the occupied north and but for very, very few they did move, some with loaded cars, others by bus and lorry. A stupendous feat, like the Israelites leaving Egypt; it took some years for the administration to function properly but surprisingly quickly, stability was achieved.

The 'border' has been maintained ever since; as foreigners we are allowed to cross over to the Greek side. Cars crossing over must be fully licensed, taxed, insured and with driving licences for both sides, and of course, changing number plates at the Greek checkpoint and vice versa we also have dual identity and registration certificates. We have very seldom spoken of leaving Cyprus. Always the question arises, where to? Kyrenia is still a delightful place, probably the most attractive in Cyprus, somewhat spoilt by a rash of ill-controlled and ill-considered building and the life style is totally different to pre-1974. We have been here a long time. 'keep busy', our personal recipe for being out to grass.

APPENDIX 1

AN EXERCISE IN HISTORY

Arthur Bryant in his *The Years of Endurance 1793 to 1802* stated in his preface:

> The British fight against the attempt of a revolutionary France to dominate the World, lasted twenty-two years. It began in 1793 when men, who had set eyes on Protector Richard Cromwell, were still living and ended in 1815 when others who were to know the youth of A. Hitler were already born.

AN INTERESTING THOUGHT!

I have often thought of my mother's association with historical events during her nearly one hundred years of living. Born in the late 1860s in outer London on a farm, she was christened Alice Louise Collins, Alice and Louise after Queen Victoria's princesses. It was customary in Britain and throughout the Empire to name children after the monarchs, millions of Georges, Edwards, Henries, Charles, etc. My middle name, Antwerp, stems from being born when my paternal uncle was killed during the Royal Marines landing in 1914 on the Belgian coast. My mother's sisters were Elizabeth, Mary and Hannah, the latter a puzzle, possibly Biblical. Her three brothers scattered around the globe. The only one we kept in touch with was James, who went to work on the Canadian Pacific Railroad and ended up President of the Grand Erie Trunk Railroad. Uncle James also I recall founded the Yellow Taxi Company in New York. So my mother's period missed the Crimean War 1853-56, between Russia and the allies, Turkey, England and France. The reason for the war was reputed to be a quarrel between Russia and France, over the Palestine Holy places, and the Russian occupation of Turkish provinces, Moldavia and Walachia. The allies curbed the Russian activities in SE Asia. Two events are paramount at the time. Florence Nightingale, The Lady with the Lamp, who railed against the intolerable nursing conditions at Scutari base hospitals and was the founder of the Royal Army Nursing Corps and the Red Cross. The other glorious event, the Charge of the Light Brigade, a stupendous act of futile gallantry, immortalised by Alfred Lord Tennyson in his poem 'The Charge of the Light Brigade'.

> Theirs not to reason why,
> Theirs but to do or die,
> Into the Valley of Death
> Rode the Six Hundred.

As an observing French general said, *'C'est magnifique, mais ce nes pas la guerre!'*
Cecil Woodham-Smith wrote a magnificent history of the episode, *The Reason Why,* from the Irish potato famine to the charge. Two garments were created at the Crimea, the Balaclava helmet, a woollen hat covering the head (used today by robbers?) and from the Earl of Cardigan, the commander-in-chief, the cardigan, button through jacket, warm woollen, very handy indoors in winter time.

The kings and queens of mother's life were many, fascinating that they all lived, reigned and died in a relatively short space of time.

Queen Victoria and her Prince Albert.
King Edward VII, bon viveur. Queen Alexandria.
King George V. The Sailor King. Queen Mary.
King Edward VIII. Abdicated. Mrs Simpson.
King George VI. A lovely King. Queen Elizabeth.
Queen Elizabeth II. Prince Philip.

So many Prime Ministers and others: Gladstone, Disraeli, Asquith, Lloyd George, Baldwin, Chamberlain, Churchill, Attlee etc.

The villains:
Kaiser Wilhelm, Queen Victoria's anathema. Hitler, Mussolini, Bismarck etc.

There followed many far-flung conquests and skirmishes: Egypt, the Sudan, the East, the conquering thin Red line, the indomitable British soldier.

Although only a small girl, my mother may have had recollections of the 1870-71, Franco-Prussian War, maybe of the French observation balloons, a first time. Bismarck goaded the French into war with Prussia. Von Moltke, a brilliant general, led the Germans to victory at the great battle of Sedan where Emperor Napoleon III was captured. Paris under seige was finally starved out in 1871. A peace treaty signed at Versailles was not at first accepted, until enforced on the French by the French army. The creation of the German Empire followed under William I of Prussia and the establishment of the Third Republic in France.

In 1878 at Rourke's Drift and Isalwanda, where three British battalions defeated some 20,000 Zulus led by Chaka their chief. Thirteen Victoria Crosses were awarded in the action, the highest award for bravery. A sergeant, VC and four soldiers from the Zulu campaign are buried here in Cyprus, part of the occupying force in 1878. The Zulu homeland is now the South African province of Natal.

South African, or Boer War, 1899-1902. Mainly caused by the Boers, the original Dutch settlers, resenting the occupation of their territories, by the British, the Transvaal and the Orange Free State. Inflamed by the influx of British settlers and prospectors, following the discovery of gold, hostilities were at first confined to raids, notably the Jameson raid in 1896, and later under Kruger, erupted into open war. Two important things occurred: the British shed their famous red coats for khaki and Baden Powell, the hero of Mafeking envisaged the Boy Scout movement, which became world wide. A guerrilla war eventually developed and such notable generals emerged, Kitchener (of Khartoum fame), Roberts, Smuts and Botha, all of whom served admirably in the Great War, then on the same side. However, the bitterness, Boer to South Africans, continues to this day, except that all appear to agree on apartheid. A famous music hall song was current in the 1900s, perhaps I can remember some of it:

> They christened the baby
> Kitchener, Kerrington,
> Keppervick, Eppervich,
> White, Kronje, Kruger,
> Palmajuba, . . .
> Cape Town, Mafeking,
> French, but not Victoria
> Babs.

I suppose Victoria Babs is the Queen, she died in 1901.

The Afghan War 1878-81. The Afghans have been fighting for many, many years and still are today, seemingly unbeatable, like the Vietnamese. The latter saw off the French in 1954 and the Americans in 1975. On their own ground, relatively undisciplined troops, such as the Turks in 1915, have generally proved unbeatable, so with the Afghans. The Afghans, clever craftsmen, used to copy the British Lee-Enfield rifle, exactly, but were unable to make the complicated, special steel bolts, for which they raided British barracks. Subsequently bolts were removed and locked up, except for the sentries' rifles. Afghan is a buffer state between Russia and British India and the conflict resulted from Anglo-Russo rivalry for influence. The British finally became a guarantor power in 1907 for the time being. Many stories have been written about the North West Frontier, the Hindu Kush and the Kyber Pass, once very popular, particularly with boys. Kipling wrote *'Barrack Room Ballads', 'Plain Tales from the Hills', 'Kim', 'Soldiers Three'*, etc.

My mother would well remember the Russo-Japanese War of 1904-05 where the Russians were surprisingly defeated mostly by naval action and the Japanese occupied the Russian ports, Port Arthur (China) and Vladivostock (Siberia). I recall the epic story of the remnants of the Russian fleet steaming an unfriendly journey across the world to Murmansk in the Arctic. Mukden was the scene of a victorious land battle where the Japanese routed the Russians. The war ended by a treaty negotiated by President Roosevelt.

The 1914-18 Great War was a tragedy for my mother, as for millions of others. Two sons killed in battle together with cousins, nephews, brothers-in-law, etc, twins died during an epidemic. That left when it was all over, two sisters and myself, my father was exempted as a civil servant. I suppose the Zeppelin raids over London were the most tiresome for the civilians. I can clearly remember nightly trips to the basement of a nearby mansion, the AA guns and silvery airships. From 1916 the Irish problem was just another thorn in the side of a tormented country. Around 1921 the Irish affair calmed down and we as children no longer fought make-believe battles with Sinn Feiners.

Between the wars we had a good life. The rise of Mussolini, Hitler, Germany arming, treaties abrogated, without much protest from the Allies, German occupation of the Rhineland, Sudetenland and finally Poland. It was not apparent to most that war was inevitable until around 1938.

1939-45. Hitler's War. Hitler's aggressive foreign policies, together with English and French appeasement, led to the war. Mussolini's adventures and conquests in 1936, Libya, Abyssinia, etc, and the Spanish Civil War helped things towards the Second World War. For my mother a grim period, her only surviving son constantly away at the wars. House bombed flat in London, domestic pets killed, for which I took deliberate revenge later. My parents moved to a pleasant small house about twenty miles from London with a surrounding garden. So life went on spending much time in the garden air-raid shelter, cold and frightened, or indoors in a steel box shelter which replaced the dining table. Fortunately buoyed up by Churchill's indomitable spirit they survived the bombs, flying bombs and rockets. Unfortunately I decided when I left the army to work in far-flung countries, with rare visits to home, much to my mother's sorrow. My father died in 1959 and I returned for my mother's terminal illness in 1960. So my mother's lifetime was centred about wars, it seems to be true that history is a record of conflicts. Heredotus, probably the first true historian, generally recorded strife between Greeks and barbarians, culminating in the Great Persian War of 480 BC, but also wrote extensively of the then known peoples of the world, Greeks, Babylonians, Egyptians, Persians, Scythians, etc. None have succeeded in writing a universal history so far, it would be a monumental task.

APPENDIX 2

THE DEMON DRINK

Alcohol and tobacco are forever in the news, the harm they do to health etc., but in spite of ever-escalating prices, the Exchequer receives more and more revenue from inveterate drinkers and smokers. My first recollection of drink was probably at the age of twelve when an old aunt, my mother's eldest sister, Hannah, gave me a cup of tea with whisky added, delicious! Aunt Hannah was a great drinker, two bottles of whisky a day even in the war, when it was scarce. She had a small copper kettle suspended over a spirit lamp, whisky and hot water on tap. However she was eighty-five when she died, so not exactly a death through alcoholism. Most of my life so far I have used alcohol habitually, beer early on, then whisky when available, Genever in West Africa, very popular with the natives, arak in Eastern countries, similar to ouzo, very pleasant when made from grapes but not so from dates when it smells like turpentine. After I retired a period of serious acquaintance with the bottle occurred, plenty of money and no responsibilities. The result a devastating experience, drinking at all hours from the bottle, not bothering with glasses. Drunken stupors, falling down and being unable to get up unaided, sick and incontinent, collapse for several days and then start again. No sex. At the time I had very vivid hallucinations unable to distinguish between fact and reality. Only the other day I asked my wife whether a certain event took place, or was it an illusion, she said, 'Yes, it did happen.' Under such circumstances one does not eat at all and my weight fell from a normal 140 lbs to 110, clothes becoming much too large. Inevitably after roughly a year of sipping on the bottle, complete collapse and being dragged unconscious to hospital. It seemed that for two days death's door was inviting me inside, but with devoted care I did not enter. There followed endless drips, mostly potassium I believe, as the body becomes denuded of this vital salt, intravenous feeding and many pills, and medicines. My liver function was reversed, anabolism and katabolism exchanged. This it appears is usually fatal, but after some weeks the reversal was stopped and I began to recover physical normality. A psychiatrist and her psychologist assistant spent some time each day of my recovery period with psychiatric examinations to establish whether brain damage had occurred, which fortunately for me had not. The sessions always began with what is the day? The date? The month? The year? – which I have always made a habit of knowing. There were trick questions, simple mental arithmetic and spelling. One exercise was to subtract mentally 7 from 100, ie 93, 7 from 93 86, etc, requires a little concentration and rhythm. There were also puzzles requiring pencil and paper. The psychiatrist's verdict was – intelligent. The outcome of this nauseating adventure, realizing that to continue would result in certain swift painful death, I gave up all forms of alcohol, there is no half-way measure. Fortunately health and strength recovered. Socially it is sometimes embarrassing not to drink, but one becomes used to that. The simple choice is to live or die a horrible death. One awful incident comes back to me, sitting on the end of the bath, violently sick into the WC and falling on my back into the bath. Alone in the house, I lay there for some three hours. An attempt to fill the bath and float out failed. Finally I managed to turn over and get on my knees. Horrible isn't it? On top of everything else one is freezing cold whatever the air temperature. Stick to soft drinks, tea and cocoa! One lasting effect concerns one's matrimonial affairs, most likely wrecked and never to be the same again. Inevitably violence occurs with one's partners, so utterly shameful and degrading. I believe that Providence has a hand in such fatal crossroads in one's life. I took to serious study aiming at a PhD by correspondence, which occupied me for over a year and this certainly helped. It is to be considered that only one alcoholic drink will start the business all over again! So don't!

I sent a copy of the above to Alcoholics Anonymous who

replied:

> 'Dear Friend, may we acknowledge with thanks receipt of your contribution to "Share". It is now being carefully read and considered for publication in our magazine. We would like you to know how much we appreciate the fact that you have taken the time and trouble to write to us. Keep well. You are a bit older than me, but that is a miracle after reading your article.
> Yours in AA
> For the Sharers.

My comment: old Providence again!
Of course some did not forget the sordidness of my behaviour, others to whom I am most grateful, were congratulatory on my unexpected recovery, attributing it to strong willpower. I do not think this is entirely true, it is rather a question of disgust with oneself and the appalling physical deterioration.

APPENDIX 3

A SECRET INTERLUDE

At one time I was recruited by a secret intelligence service. How? Certainly by background investigation, not difficult these days with so much form filling and inevitable records in various countries where engaged in projects, sometimes government sponsored. The proposal was to act as a courier, go-between, shall we say, of the sources of information and the agent. It was so odd that the jargon employed in these activities was identical to that to be found in spy stories. Drops, in cafés, sometimes in the street, kiosks, safe houses, once via a dustbin. The methods of communication varied, usually very clever devices and codes were employed. A safe house, or flat, was one with a concealed or not easily observed entrance, where one could park a car unobtrusively and approach on foot. Instinctively one never asked questions. The source was naturally at risk and the courier very much so, both to be disowned and punished, of course, if caught. The agent always had diplomatic cover and a plausible position such as Cultural Secretary, if found out – expulsion as we all know.

My part was unrewarded and of course not acknowledged in any way. For the courier it was an awfully lonely life, none to confide in. The agents were as far as I know always recruited from universities such as Oxford, Yale or the Sorbonne, it appears that there is no other method of entry, I did try in 1948 without success. The engineer or surveyor using a theodolite is frequently suspect of spying in the more backward countries (the Arabic for spy and theodolite is synonymous). In Iraq I was once arrested and taken handcuffed to the nearest police barracks which happened to be in

Hillah at Babylon. Fortunately I was on a government new road project and was released. In Iraq the particular contractor's name displayed in bright yellow on all plant and vehicles, was very similar to Wazir in Arabic script, so we were thought to belong to the Crown Prince. Iraq was at the time a Hashemite Kingdom.

The interlude ended in dead silence, no explanation, just *finis*. Absolute security all round for, who will put one's head on the block?

An interesting experience, but very frightening.

LIST OF ILLUSTRATIONS

My Mother and some of her children in the village school playground. 11
3rd Royal Tanks badge. 27
Map of the Theatre – North Africa 30
M-13 Italy light recce tank 1940. 36
Map of the Western desert. 47
Sherman Mark V (USA) tank 1942. 52
Grant Medium M3 (USA) tank 1941. 53
Stuart M3 Mark I (USA) tank 1940. 53
Crusader Cruiser Mark I (Britain) tank 1939. 54
The 40 ton Churchill Infantry tank. 54
Line ahead on Salisbury Plain. 55
The Sherman in Normandy 1944. 56
PZKW Mark IIIA (Germany) tank 1938. 57
PZKW Mark IVE (Germany) tank 1941. 57
Panther D (Germany) tank 1942. 57
The officers before Alamein. 59
Cairo 1942 Identity card photo. 60
Map – on to Tunis 1942-43. 66
Sherman Firefly tank. 77
1944 Aldershot. The officers. 78
Map of Normandy. 80
1944 Leicester Royal Infirmary 'Jessie Matthews'. 86
1945 Berlin. Recovered Dutch paintings – my reward. 91
1947 Germany. Flensburg. 94
Map of The Gulf. 99
1948 Bahrain. The refinery and the Virgins Pool. 101
Map of The Middle East. 110
1954 Iraq – The Burning Bush; 1956 Iraq – Lala Ali Khan. 113

1953 Iraq – Kut Road; 1954 Iraq – Trade Fair; 1954 Iraq – Sesidi Temple Mosul.	119
1956 Iraq Mosul.	129
Map of oil pipe line, India.	134
Map of The West African Coast.	135
1960 Iran – Agha Jari airfield.	142
1961 Libya – Tripoli's British bank.	146
1964 Libya – British bank Benghazi.	149
1965 Guinea – Textile complex.	153
The British Embassy staff leaving after breaking off diplomatic relations.	156
1948 Jordan – King Hussein Military Hospital ward blocks; 1968 Jordan – The Mosque; 1969 Jordan – King Hussein Military Hospital entrance.	163
Roman ruins – many remain in Jordan.	165
1970-73 Abu Dhabi Hilton; 1971 Abu Dhabi – French made armoured car.	169
Maps of Egypt and Cyprus.	173
1974 Cyprus – Turkish memorial.	176
HMS *Liverpool* missile cruiser.	177